Empath

Guide For Highly Sensitive People To Deal With Psychopaths and Narcissists and Energy Vampires

(Learn To Open Your Third Eye and Kundalini Awakening)

Jacob Barlow

Published By **Zoe Lawson**

Jacob Barlow

All Rights Reserved

Empath: Guide For Highly Sensitive People To Deal With Psychopaths and Narcissists and Energy Vampires (Learn To Open Your Third Eye and Kundalini Awakening)

ISBN 978-1-77485-679-6

No part of this guidebook shall be reproduced in any form without permission in writing from the publisher except in the case of brief quotations embodied in critical articles or reviews.

Legal & Disclaimer

The information contained in this ebook is not designed to replace or take the place of any form of medicine or professional medical advice. The information in this ebook has been provided for educational & entertainment purposes only.

The information contained in this book has been compiled from sources deemed reliable, and it is accurate to the best of the Author's knowledge; however, the Author cannot guarantee its accuracy and validity and cannot be held liable for any errors or omissions. Changes are periodically made to this book. You must consult your doctor or get professional medical advice before using any of the suggested remedies, techniques, or information in this book.

Upon using the information contained in this book, you agree to hold harmless the Author from and against any damages, costs, and expenses, including any legal fees potentially resulting from the application of any of the information provided by this guide. This disclaimer applies to any damages or injury caused by the use and application, whether directly or indirectly, of any advice or information presented, whether for breach of contract, tort, negligence, personal injury, criminal intent, or under any other cause of action.

You agree to accept all risks of using the information presented inside this book. You need to consult a professional medical practitioner in order to ensure you are both able and healthy enough to participate in this program.

Table Of Contents

Chapter 1: Understanding The Enigma Called An Empath _____ 1

Chapter 2: Protecting Yourself From Negativity: Exercises To Stop The Dripping. _____ 16

Chapter 3: What Is An Empath? ___ 35

Chapter 4: The Sensitive Disorder _ 56

Chapter 5: Benefits And The Challenges Of Being An Empath __ 79

Chapter 6: The Dark Side Of Empaths _____ 91

Chapter 7: How To End The Emotional Overload _____ 98

Chapter 8: What Can You Tell Whether Your Empath? _____ 117

Chapter 9: Signs That You Might Be Psychic And The Describe The Exercise To Learn About It _____ 135

Chapter 10: The Complete Guide To Know About Psychic Protection __155

Chapter 11: Stabilize , And Sustain Your Gift _____ 174

Chapter 1: Understanding The Enigma Called An Empath

Empaths are a normal part of life. Empath is normal

The world we live in has a strong desire for normal things. It is a rigid worldview of everything being rational and normal and everything that isn't in line with these standards is considered unusual.

When you meet with others generally, it is the norm to engage in conversation. If you don't, something that is considered to be unusual as well as socially insecure.

* Our species has always felt more at ease in groups. Feeling uncomfortable or insecure within groups could be categorized as being abnormal or uncomfortable.

* We love to be in crowds, pretending to be sociable with other people, yet hide our true feelings or state of mind. But, it is

interesting that if anyone can sense these emotions or feel them, we feel at risk or frightened. One could also consider such an individual abnormal.

Abnormal is a term that the world has come up with to define anything that is out of normal range of comprehension or the average person's reach. It's the category in which empaths typically fall.

Empaths are not unusual. Empaths are also just similar to any other human anywhere in the world. The difference is that empaths have special abilities that are not shared by others and, sometimes, that individual is unable to fully comprehend the power and abilities.

Who is an Empath?

You're an empath if you are able to comprehend and take in the emotional or mental condition of people around you. You will have to be cautious in understanding the word carefully. A majority of people are competent to make an educated assumption about another's emotional or mental state. Certain people might even be able to speak to them with a clear and direct manner. But, only a few who have a unique ability to feel deeply can sense the emotional or mental state inside themselves. These people can empathize. They not only comprehend the pain that others feel but they also feel that hurt deep inside themselves.

The person who is able to be emphatic in order that they can build stronger relationships with others. Empaths will develop with sensitivities that assist them to feel emotional, pain and feelings of discomfort felt by other people.

Being an empath is an emotional rollercoaster. Empaths are sensitive to the feelings of others around them, and their moods can have a huge impact on the person they are. It can be an overwhelming experience for empaths, and can cause an empath shy of crowds or exposure to public. A person who has a lack of control over their gift could be more difficult to interact with large numbers as the energy surrounding the empath are constantly affecting the person even when they are not talking to people who have such power.

Empaths are highly sensitive persons. They feel emotions, pain, and energy of others much more strongly. But, the issue does not end there. Certain empaths who have strong sensitivities and very permeable boundaries may not just be aware of them, but they also start to absorb them. It could be a problem when they are a repository of all negativity, stress and stress.

Thus, an empath could be a person who has the ability to see at the innermost parts of the mind of an individual within the front, and beyond the surface. Empaths with this kind of ability are able to play an important role in helping others because they are healers with a gift.

An empath may also be someone who cannot manage the quantity of negative energy that is leaking into and thus is are forced to live with unending pain and discomfort.

They are only two aspects that make an empath. Contrary to what the majority of people think empaths are not a curse or an advantage; it's simply a condition of increased sensibilities as well as the degree of control and understanding that one has over their surroundings.

Some empaths could have sensitive to a lesser degree and might not be affected by it too much. While others may have high sensitivities. And they might feel overwhelmed for a long time, if they haven't built up the boundaries of their own.

No matter what degree of sensitivities you possess the fact that you are an empath is not a problem. If you've never developed control over your emotions it is possible that you be overwhelmed by negative thoughts as well as thoughts and emotions. It's not uncommon to be averse to places that are crowded. This is very feasible and is typical. However, this isn't what it is going to remain forever.

The empath is able to make use of this ability to detect people's behavior and gain a profound understanding of human psychology.

A few of the most powerful features that can make life for empaths difficult. However, empaths can be able to handle the situation if is able to manage their powers effectively.

An empath isn't an obnoxious or a magician. The empath is like the rest of us and a human being with certain talents that an empath is able to make sharper and use to heal others. If the empath is unable to see the gifts, they may become thorns and begin causing lots of trouble within.

Boons as well as Banes of an Empath

Empaths' character traits can vary and I haven't chosen the most effective in this article because the majority of empaths do not possess all of them in common. These are four traits which are typically common to the majority of empaths. They must be considered carefully in order to avoid them, or they may become even more threatening.

Intuitive

This is by far the most well-known and easily understood characteristic of empaths. Every person has a certain amount of intuition. The instinctual feeling inside us warns us about dangers and steers us to avoid them. This instinctual feeling is the best option in almost all circumstances for us. But empaths also have an innate talent for intuition. They are extremely sensitive capable of listening to their own inner thoughts when they have to judge the actions of others with care. It is easy for them to differentiate between positive and negative energies within people because they feel them in their own body.

Future events are the direct consequence of the actions taken in the present. The ability to sense the future of anyone can aid in determining the future. Since empaths have an obvious advantage in this field they are more adept in predicting the future.

But, this extraordinary ability can be detrimental to empaths who do not maintain control over their capacities and their emotions. Empaths are extremely sensitive and are able to quickly be enticed to isolate themselves from the rest of the world to prevent the negative energy flow which can aid them in being able to sense.

Some empaths could also start depending on other inputs such as dreaming, psychic inputs or precognitive abilities. They may also be able to sense the sensations they experience around them. this could also boost their abilities to perceive.

These are all abilities that empaths are able to use when they've realized their potential. Empaths may not be in a position to appreciate all of these potentialities, and some might not be able to master each of them, however they are able to take advantage of the many possibilities available to them to make use of.

Recognizing the potential of intuition can be achieved quickly to the empath since the sensitivities are extremely high. But, it's an ability that must be developed by practicing and focusing on your gut feeling. It's also the ability to assist empaths in forming strong bonds.

The majority of empaths are susceptible to energy vampires which can deplete them of their emotional energy, leaving the person feeling exhausted. People's toxic behavior who are around you can start stressing their bodies, minds and emotionally.

The ability to discern can aid empaths in avoiding certain individuals and situations. However, all empaths might not be able to use the capacity to discern in the same way. However, empaths can enhance the power of intuition being an empath is always beneficial.

Intense

An empath's status doesn't come without a few hurdles and being in a state of intenseness is among the many. An empath is a person who is able to feel things more strongly than other people. This means that something that might be even a single thought in the brain of an individual may make an empath shake.

As an example, we see numerous unfortunate individuals and creatures as we drive by. Many people do not look around because they are working or busy. However, this might not be the case for empaths. Empaths can be deeply distressed at the sight or presence of people like these around. If helping these people is not feasible the hurt and pain can remain in the soul of an empath.

Similar to that empaths may experience other emotions such as trust and love with a great deal of intensity and might be injured more than other people.

Uncentered

Another battle empaths may need to fight for their entire life. Empaths might not be at ease all the times. There's always an underlying feeling in the back of your mind that something is not in the norm or something isn't quite right.

This anxiety stems from the constant influence of energy from outside empaths keep getting that causes the unsettling sensation.

It's not a characteristic or a gift, or curse, it's just a characteristic that empaths generally display.

Perplexed

For an empath that is not awakened it's not unusual to feel confused all the times. Empaths live in constant agony being a victim of the things they don't want or need around them. They are affected by the feelings of their friends and are stricken with grief and angst. They are not able to establish personal boundaries and are unable to the separation of feelings between others and their own, keeps becoming more and more complicated for them. It could be the pain of encounter with large crowds, or the satisfaction of being in a secluded space Empaths who aren't awake are a struggle whatever the reason. The struggle between guilt and pain is never ending.

But, it's not the only experience available to every empath. A fully awake empath is aware of the art of controlling their emotions. They have a set of personal limits that allow them to feel the emotions of others without becoming lost in them.

A mature empath will know how to avoid becoming lost in the issue when trying to resolve it. This isn't a skill can be acquired as a default. It's something that empaths need to master and master.

Most people have bizarre notions about empaths. The majority of their information comes from fiction that is exaggerated and that is portrayed in the idiot box as well as in the literature of leisure.

Empaths aren't an exclusive breed , or mutants possessing advanced abilities. Many people are born with above average sensitiveness. They feel emotions with more intensities than others.

It's true empaths have a greater sense of intuition and perception, however, that doesn't mean they are fortune-tellers. Every coin comes with two sides, as being an empath not an exception.

Unawakened empaths with weak boundaries could live an existence of pain and suffering. There is no escape for these empaths since they can feel lost throughout the day. The ability to discern between their own feelings and the emotions that others perceive might be weakened. There may be no escape from the constant flood of emotions they don't understand and this can be detrimental to their mental, emotional, and physical well-being.

Contrary to what is commonly believed empaths are not a fairytale. It's simply a weak and troubled physical and psychological state for an empath.

But, that could be altered for an awakened empath who is in control of his/her senses. An awakened and confident empath might not be able to anticipate the future or understand the minds of the people in his vicinity. However, they do be able to judge individuals by the first impression they leave behind by them.

A properly functioning empath would also possess the ability to sense and thus would have greater control over situations.

Being an empath isn't an oasis of flowers or an edgy seat. It's a skill with which you were born. It's not something that's going to disappear in time, and the act of ignoring it won't aid. If you don't think about it long enough it could cause you to feel anxious as well as fear, anger and pain. It can also cause discord. But, if you focus to develop your talent and develop it, you might not just be able to be aware of your abilities but also assist others who are around you.

Chapter 2: Protecting Yourself From Negativity: Exercises To Stop The Dripping.

Techniques for Protection in the Middle of all Doubters.

Making sure you are safe from the drain isn't something most people are aware of.

The term"energy vampire" has been circulating in recent years. People have been talking about the issue in the media, on Oprah as well as TED talks, as well as in their homes and spas. It is evident that something needs to be done for the benefit of our energy and relationships are dependent on it. What is an energy savage and how do you take precautions to protect yourself? Narcissists, as we discussed previously in chapter are self-absorbed people who draw their egos from others. The job of an energy vampire is similar as that of the energy vampire: to draw energy from those around them due to their ability as well as to push the boundaries. They draw energy from you to test the extent to which they are able to drain before you allow your guard to fall.

Like narcissists and narcissists not all energy vampires know they are able to do this, however they do have some, and, like the narcissists, profit from the circumstance. In addition to the obvious feeling that your energy is being depleted and drained, especially if you're an empath (what color of cape did pick?) There are several indicators you need to be aware of in addition to the signs that we've already mentioned. Wow, there's lots of attention to be paid on. Keep in mind that you can look for the positive things around you too.

Many people who be a believer in the hard evidence do not believe in the existence of energy vampires. It doesn't mean the energy vampire doesn't exist, it's just not acknowledged by everyone. In the event that an energy vampire were to go to a gathering of non-believers the only thing guests could notice is their narcissism not their capabilities to be an energy vampire who draws energy from others surrounding them. People might not believe that this is possible, and likely claim that they feel exhausted due to fatigue and tired, if they even notice even noticing. This makes it hard for guests to safeguard themselves. It is impossible to defend yourself from something if you don't even know that it exists. This is similar to sunscreen. People who do not believe in or are unaware of the risks of sun exposure and sun damage will never apply sunscreen. Party guests who aren't convinced are likely to ignore warnings, and the possible damage caused by the energy vampire goes under the radar.

Energy vampires aren't usually those who sit in the corner and observe from a distance. They must be active because, in general energy vampires are full of energy (not to be confused with ego , which was discussed in the earlier chapter) however, their energy can be disorienting and scattered due to the fact that they struggle with controlling their emotions and perform behaviors that are linked to their moods. This means that those who are energy vampires, which we'll name her Eve is likely to behave awkwardly when around people she does not know. Eve is known to be overreactive due to feelings of mixed emotions. She always seeks an opportunity to sit down to process her emotions that aren't quite right. If Eve were to have been at Nat's birthday celebration, she would follow her own rules but would have ignored social etiquette and subtle cues that could make the guests feel uncomfortable. The way people react to one another is a great indicator that an energy savage may be in the vicinity since people react subconsciously that allows their instincts and previous experience to influence their thinking and actions.

If you observe that you have a competitive energy vampire you may choose to ignore their competitive nature and ignore them to protect yourself. If you don't react to their competitive nature, you're getting rid of the chance for the person who is competitive in her energy to boast about her accomplishments. Most people don't know how to respond when bragging is excessive However, this method of protection can be very useful, even if your friends think that excessive competitiveness is good for you.

The energy vampires who are competitive and try to beat each tale you share are "me too" energy vampires. If you've got an old family tale about an excursion to Europe and South America, then the'me to' energy vampire is likely to have traveled to Europe or South America. If Eve interrupts the conversation with her own experiences and speaks to Rath and you Rath You might think of your reaction to be an argument between the two of you to determine which one has the most compelling story however this could create a worse situation. When you are absorbed in the epic energy vampire stories, you're allowing yourself to be swept up in their fantasies, and which can drain your energy and keep you caught up in a beautiful story. It is possible to be politely interrupting Eve and inform her that you're conducting a private discussion and that you will talk with her following the conversation or at another moment if you're worried that the contest could consume more energy than you're ready to commit.

Being able to protect yourself from manipulative flattery and gifts isn't something you can do easily or be able to master without having been in a long-term relationship with the energy vampires or narcissists. Strategies for protection include recognizing the gifts and flatteries as it is: trick to distract you from the subject that is at hand. If you tell the doting energy vampire that you won't be purchased, they will lose a lot of influence within their own thinking. Their facade is ruined and for someone who has emotional and physical imbalances they'll likely be foolish and won't be a bother ever again.

To safeguard yourself from anyone who is overreactive and communicates in a confusing manner You could say in a calm manner that you haven't had a good night's sleep and aren't feeling well due to it. Reacting aggressively at the smallest annoyance is exhausting, but to say it in a way that this could be perceived as rude. The act of telling Eve that you don't need to speak because you've been occupied for the past week, and you'd like to take a moment to yourself an easy way to say "OMG you're draining me more than a pump for a swimming pool!" As long as Eve cannot read your mind then you're good to go and she'll probably go on and move on to another person. The Debby Downers are victims due to their negative attitude; they do not often have the ability to see the bright ending of the tunnel. They may not even be able to see the tunnel within the abyss they've encased themselves in. To shield yourself from the energy vampire, begin setting limits regarding the amount of negativity you are willing to allow. You should try to steer the conversation to an optimistic tone and concentrate on this. When Dee Dee insists on ignoring the positive aspect it is possible to take a break or request her to indulge in the positive side for just a short period of time for a test out. Maybe the energy vampire could become exposed to an kind of optimism that will assist them in changing the way they approach things.

Construction of the necessary Walls and barriers to safeguard yourself from Energy Vampires.

The energy vampires can be very draining you when they look at every aspect as a contest. They'll do it in their own manner and most of the time they'll be doing it secretly so that it is difficult to know what they lose. This type of attitude puts those who are on defense. lacking experience in these kinds of contests can make you feel uncomfortable which can make you feel less than Eve even if this occurs in the presence of others. If you do something well and you are proud of it the energy vampire with a competitive streak will minimize your accomplishments and draw attention back to them. One of the indicators for an energy vulture is the refusal to accept the responsibility of their actions because they are distracted by the people around them. A little pizazz and a small gift can are a great way to show that they wish to distract your attention from the primary concept or the most important concern. How often has your partner returned home with chocolates and flowers following a major argument? He tried to divert you from the negative feelings that you felt towards him at the moment. The same thing happens with energy vampires. They are able to keep you away from the issue in front of them so that they don't have to accept the responsibility for their actions.

Being able to deal with energy vampires may be challenging, especially when avoiding them isn't an alternative. Avoiding them is the recommendation of psychiatrists and psychologists, however, in reality, it's not always the best option.

The key thing to remember is to ensure you have a strong support system that isn't being offered by the energy vampires within your life. You also need to build walls and barriers to shield yourself. The construction of a wall within your head to prevent negative energy and the insanity will aid you in dealing to Eve as well as any energy vampires that you encounter.

It's your party , and everybody is present: family, friends, Nat, Aqua, Eve, Mic and Rath and you're having a blast. You're sitting with Eve who is making fun of the topic of her conversation (again) then you begin feeling exhausted. Are you feeling the effects of alcohol? Did you get enough sleep? You realize Eve is taking your attention as you speak and you realize that you need to stop her in some way, or else you may have to be excused to lay down. This isn't the way the hostesses with the most ought to do at her private celebration.

What are you going to do? Being an empath who doesn't know ways to stop this flow could make your life challenging for sure. Luckily, you are aware of the tips.

Breathing is a crucial aspect of stopping the power that the vampire uses to drain your energy or your emotions. It is true that breathing is essential for many other reasons as well however, there are many other books to help you with that. If you're not able to get away from Eve and her negative thoughts, paying attention to your breathing can assist you. If you're taking your breath (whether you are aware of whether or not) then you won't be in a position to let go of the negative feelings Eve is bringing , and it will create tension. It is likely that you won't be able to let the tension go until everyone is gone. This isn't a good scenario. Keep your eyes on your breathing, and focus on your lungs, no matter how large or small and feel your breath move through and out, into and out, and in and out. When you concentrate on your breathing by doing this, you're taking control of the amount of energy Eve can steal. You're gaining back the energy. Walls against other people may seem a little odd initially, but it's crucial to determine that the person or event does not interfere with your mental health or wellbeing.

How to choose who you spend your time with also helps.

If Eve attends the event, she would make sure she's The Belle of the Ball, like the way Nat and Aqua would make sure that all focus is on the two of them. This event is turning into more me-centered do you not think? In the event that you attended the gathering and were talking about Rath about your favourite movies or childhood memories, Eve would interject and engage in a conversation about her. The narcissistic, energy vampire connection is more obvious today isn't it? Eve is going to make it all about her. Her charismatic nature will cause everyone to be a part of the fun and have fun with her as if this was her own party and you should not forget the experience.

Energy vampires aren't positive people, and they will take every occasion to criticize anything even if it may be. They'll also be angry if you attempt to portray yourself as a voice of optimism. They believe that everything is bound to fail. How do you make positive change to failure? The term "vampire" is appropriate in this situation since Eve attempts to pull the joy and optimism from the conversation to substitute it with her negativity. Beware of this person. It may not be the best choice as it could be your first experience with an energy vampire.

Have you been to an event where guests had a good time but then discover the group's leaders have used your curious nature to gain advantage, knowing that you'll feel excluded if they engage in an uninvolved conversation? The energy vampire within the group is fully aware of this, and they have turned your personality against you, and to benefit themselves. This is because they've controlled the situation, and believed that you wouldn't know how to fight them. If you're a caring and compassionate individual, as is the norm with empaths, then the energy vampire can use this to harm you, too. The energy vampire will make use of your affection for other people for their own gain, and will eventually be the new friend you've been looking for realizing that you're not a good enough person to let them down.

Excuses are a typical strategy used by energy vampires, and is closely related to their fear of accountability. When they excuse themselves, and continue to make excuses, they are able to avoid accountability for their actions and choices. Eve is a victim, she loves to play and, as long as she complains the problem will eventually be worked out (in her mind). When Eve is more comfortable making excuses and being adamant about the inability of her to alter anything the problem gets worse. Eve loves to lure people into her fantasies to make it appear acceptable if she just leaves things in the same state. This could be detrimental since Eve will always find reasons to avoid responsibility.

This method of avoiding, as well as numerous other reasons discussed previously in the chapter is a good reminder of the people you choose to spend your time with. If you're an energy-hungry person in your life, spend time with people who will bring you back to your feet (no you don't need to turn to your parents for grounding) and help you to be focused on something else than the exhausting and mixed energy of vampires is a method to combat the effects of Eve that is in your life.

What are the tricks that the sensitive Empath can apply.

There are a few who enjoy moving. It's stressful, is expensive, and it can make you freak Frou Frou off. Refusing to leave the energy vampire can be just as stressful. it can take time as you could have to find an area to keep yourself from being a burden and also, time is money, after all. Even though removing yourself from Eve isn't likely in the moment, this could be the only alternative. Away from Eve and being around empaths is an effective method to reduce the amount of time you spend with those whom drain your energies. If you make a move toward Rath and any empaths, your drain will cease and instead Rath as well as her fellow empaths will boost your energy because that's the nature of empaths. They are generous without asking any reward and are able to help people in need in their own capacity to help others.

Removing yourself from Eve is not the only step in order to be free of your energy draw. The idea of moving to a more private space to relax can be as simple as breathing in a healthy way, as we have previously described. It could also involve other activities like focusing on positive thought or reminiscing about an enjoyable and healthy relationship or imagining the best memories that you had in your early years. What do you notice or smell? Is the scent of your husband's perfume to the max? What is your bestie's stunning garden? to find peace after you've come across the energy vampire, it will give your peace and will not cause you to feel as if your mind is a mess.

Many empaths like hand-holding and hugging since it assists them in connecting with people who are around them. However there are some empaths who like to keep their distance due to this reason. There isn't any one trick that a empath with sensitivity to employ to limit your contact with people who are energy vampires as well as negative people generally is a great way to reduce the quantity of negative energy that you're exposed. It might seem unfair when you're around those who require this physical contact, for instance, when you visit relatives or a grieving relative for instance. However, if you're exhausted in the first hour of your visit, you'll be unable to comfort someone or anyone else afterward.

It's great to spend time outdoors among the bugs and plants--is it is a spider? No, I'm going to the inside -- is not just beneficial for the plants empath. Grounding is a brand new concept which connects you to the earth by using your feet and mud, grass, and more. Due to the earth's healing properties and natural healing properties, taking time to center yourself is a technique can be done in the event of a emotional or sensory overload due to Eve or another energy vampires in your life. The best place to ground yourself could include any grassy , areas of sandy soil, ground covered with rocks, soil, or mossy soil, similar to the forest. Any ground that isn't contaminated by technology or buildings will work. If you reside in an apartment or flat apartment that doesn't have a garden, you could purchase the tub and fill it up with these substances, then step into the tub for therapeutic grounding. If you decide to use this method ensure that you wash the soil, sand or any other material. regularly to avoid absorbing all negative energy, and then let it out to your house. You can also purchase an earthing mat online retailers however I'm not sure what polyurethane is compared with the natural beauty.

These techniques can be utilized by any person, but they are particularly beneficial for people who have a sensitive sensitivity to the harsh environment of our current time. The most important thing and what makes these strategies be effective for you is your determination and persistence to improve your empathic skills while also helping others who are around you. If you attempt one of these methods make sure you be aware of the reason you're doing these actions and why they can benefit you as a person. When using these strategies it is crucial to realize that you're unlikely to fail if you have faith in the methods and trust in yourself. Believe in yourself, trust your guts, and empathize. They are there to do it for a reason.

Chapter 3: What Is An Empath?

An empath is someone with an open mind; both in the unobserved and perceived world, they do not perceive things to the point that they could become burdensome. Empaths absorb energy that is affecting them and have the ability to react to others' emotions. They are influenced by the moods and emotions, as well as the expectations and desires of others. Being an empath doesn't limit them to heightened sensitivity or emotions They are aware of the motives and motives of others instinctively. Empath isn't something you can learn or taught; you either are born that way or do not. Being an empath, you are constantly in touch with the emotions of others and their thoughts, making sure that you're always carrying the burden of others who surround you.

Physical manifestations of emotions they carry the way they feel, like constant pain and discomfort, and chronic fatigue, are susceptible to multiple empathy. You've surely were familiar with the phrase, "You look like you're carrying all the burden of the universe!" That's what the empath does! They carry all the power and emotions as well as their karma, which they come into contact with. Empaths are extremely humble; they avoid compliments, and often prefer to give them to someone else than accepting them. They speak with great energy and express themselves with a lot of honesty which often causes the offence. They're not people who conceal their feelings and will be open to anyone who's willing to listen.

They could even be to the other side of this. They can be extremely antisocial and be adamant to block people they feel are preventing their progress in any way from their lives. They don't know what motivates them to do this; it is also a way of removing the emotional burdens and energy they constantly confront from other people to the empath who might not know their identity.

While empaths are sensitive to others' feelings however, they spend little time paying attention to their own heart. They may be influenced by their own interests to consider the requirements of other people. The majority of empaths are non-violent, non-aggressive and swiftly becomes the peacemaker among people. If they're in an environment of conflict an empath is very uncomfortable. They try to tend to avoid conflict or change their behavior swiftly if the situation becomes out of hand. They are ashamed of themselves and are quick to issue an apology if they are unable to control the situation and make a statement that could be offensive to others.

Empaths seem to pick up their surroundings' feelings and transmit them to the person, without fully understanding the reason behind their actions. When an empath has reached the initial stages of discovering their gifts, it is recommended that they speak things out to ease the accumulation of emotions. If not, they'll prefer to keep things inside and construct walls of tall buildings around them, and refuse to let people into their world. Inability to express their emotions is usually result of a traumatizing event, or the childhood when emotions weren't spoken in the home, or by parents who told them to be aware of and not listen to their emotions.

The emotional detachment of people can have an adverse effect on our health. The more they control us, the more we hold our emotions in without letting them go. There will be a release as the feelings build up and this release is an excellent thing. Humans are taught to express himself whenever there is a need and that's how healing takes place. When you share your thoughts there is a feeling of relief that you aren't carrying the burden alone. There's a risk of emotional and mental unstable as and negative emotions that can manifest as an illness should this not occur.

Empaths are sensitive to films images, television and news programmes that feature scenes of violence, or physical or emotional anxiety, whether adult or child. They can be dragged to tears and make them become physically sick. If they don't possess the same level of human compassion as we do, they find it difficult to articulate the pain they feel, as having little tolerance.

Empaths have careers which encourage them, be it working with animals, nature or with people, to help others. They are enthusiastic about their job and what they contribute to the world. Empaths also have volunteer positions that commit their time and energy to helping others with no pay or recognition. Empaths are great storytellers due to their unending imagination. They are constantly inquiring as well as asking the right questions. They are also very kind and romantic. They are devoted to their family's heritage and are able to keep old memories, jewellery, or other treasures handed down through generations. They are often the ones who listen to the stories of their grandparents and great grandparents . They also are armed with knowledge about their family's history.

They are able to listen to a variety of styles of music to suit their moods. experiencing. People are usually interested in their musical tastes particularly the amount of variety. They can listen to music from classical for just one minute and then they switch to they are listening to a hardcore music, they're rapping! The lyrics of songs can be a significant influence on empaths, particularly when it is related to an event they've just experienced. To avoid sending their emotions to a high it is suggested empaths to listen to music with no lyrics.

Empaths employ bodies as a method of expression. Through movement, dance and even acting in a way, they communicate in a way that is as easy as communicating by using words. Empaths, when they dance, can demonstrate high levels of energy and get lost in the music, and then enter an almost trance state when their bodies move with the beat as well as the lyrics. They describe this as being completely disoriented; they're no longer aware of their surroundings.

Empaths are beautiful, which is why people naturally gravitate towards them, but they don't know the reason. They are able to see that complete strangers are comfortable with sharing intimate topics and conversations with them. Another reason that empaths are so enticing is that it is a good listeners. It's lively energetic, outgoing and they want to be around. They are the heart and heart of any group, and due to their energy, people love to surround them. This is not only due to the intense nature of their personality Their moods change instantly and they will disperse like cockroaches to stay clear of them. The burden of carrying multiple emotions can be overwhelming if someone who empathizes with them cannot recognize their talents. They don't know what they feel when they experience the feelings of another person and it can be difficult for them. They can be happy for a moment , and then the next they feel a swell of depression, which triggers them to get angry.

It's not a good idea to give up empathy during one of their mood swings that occur in the heights. Anybody who's around during this moment should offer the person a shoulder to cry and listen, and keep an ear open. Sometimes, this kind of intense emotional attention can bring about a swift healing. Empaths are frequently misguided and it's the most important element of their journey they along with those who surround them, don't only know themselves.

Empaths also learn and problem solvers They are also avid researchers and love exploring various kinds of. They believe that there are both problems and solutions that are in sync and that the solution is always within reach.

Sometimes, they look around until they discover the answer to a problem, which can provide great assistance to their fellow workers in their work environment and at home. Empaths are also capable of tapping into information from the universe and seeking out advice to resolve the issue they've set the issue in their mind.

Empaths are dreamers. Their dreams are rich and informative. They think that their dreams are linked to their real life, and that what is taking place in their life or in the lives of those who they care about is advised about. They've invested their time and energy since childhood in finding the secret to their dreams.

Empaths thrive on mental stimulation They have no need to be a part of the world and find it difficult to focus on things that don't inspire them. They may also turn to daydreaming, and eventually fall into a state of disconnection from the mind when they feel they are being bored. While their body is at the same level but they also have a dimension of their minds.

If they're as well-educated and emotionally strong as they appear an instructor can only keep the interest of an emotional student. If not they'll be turned off effortlessly. If their audience isn't able to completely captivate them and they aren't interested. Because of their ability to become so consumed in the feelings other people, they create the most effective actors. When they take on a role they perform it by expressing the entire emotion that characterize the person they are playing.

They are susceptible to synchronicities and the feeling of deja vu that is being observed. The initial sequence of synchronicities that continue to occur can lead to an understanding of the person who empathizes to perceive the future. Once this understanding is realized, and they begin to speak with the potential of their gift. an euphoric feeling is felt.

A lot of empaths have a deep connection to the supernatural; all their life, they might experience a myriad of near-death experiences and other out-of-body experiences. Being transported to another dimension of the spirit world is a normal occurrence for empaths. They are free spirits , and what they are looking for isn't the everyday routine of everyday life. When they find themselves in this cycle, their feeling of living is gone and they are compelled to take a breather, reflect on their lives, and come back to self-discovery in their journey. The experiences that they experience through paranormal means contribute to the feeling of being isolated. This isn't typical for everyone empaths are more likely to restrict their abilities for the fear of being unfairly stigmatized. However, they are able to overcome this issue, and typically happens when they are in the presence of other empaths.

There are several empaths with unique psychic emphatic attribute. The following are the exact definitions:

Geomancy: Geomancers possess the ability to sense the energy of the earth. they feel the energy when on specific land or in certain locations. They experience headaches whenever a natural catastrophe is about to happen regardless of the location the location it occurs.

Telepathy: They possess the ability to listen to others minds.

Psychometry: They could draw energy from their images, perceptions, places or even artifacts.

Physical Healing: ability to feel within their bodily body, the physiological effects experienced by others, and later use to help heal.

Communicating with animals is the ability to hear, sense and communicate with animals.

Healing through emotion: The ability to feel the feelings of others.

Nature: The ability to connect with nature and plants.

Mediumship Ability to perceive spirits' presence as well as their presence.

Awareness or claircognizanceis the capability to know what has to be performed in any given circumstance when in the midst of a crisis, this ability is usually paired with an underlying sense of calm and tranquility.

Precognition The ability to sense that an important happening is coming. Also, there is a feeling of gloom or anxiety that is enigmatic.

If you're not sure about whether you possess an empathic gift There are 25 common traits of empaths:

They're looking for the person who has survived, the weaker or those suffering from mental illness and suffering are attracting the attention of empaths.

The empath is highly imaginative with an enthralling imagination. The ability to dance, sing and draw, perform, or write is often multitalented. A messy world full of chaos and confusion hinders the flow of energy that empaths have The empaths are minimalist and tidy.

They don't care about self-importance. Though empaths are extremely tolerant and compassionate They aren't keen to be with people who live solely for themselves. They have no regard for the feelings and feelings.

In the food they eat, they feel the energy. Empaths are also vegetarians because the pain suffered by animals when they are killed can be felt.

They aren't keen on buying second-hand goods, since they believe that their energy is absorbed by something that's owned by someone else. They prefer to purchase an entirely new home or a brand-new car as long as the investment can be financially secured, so that they aren't entangled in someone else's energy.

They can be found daydreaming for hours. An empath's imagination could get lost; they are able to stare for hours in oblivion. They are bored and disengaged when the empath isn't being stimulated. Be it at home, work, or in school, they must be actively engaged in their work or else they'll wander.

They seek out information. Empaths are still learning something new and if they're faced with unanswered questions, they will find it difficult, and will go above and beyond their obligation to discover the solution. They'll look for confirmation whenever they sense the nudge within their soul that they know the answer. The drawback to it is the fact that they have many different information that could be exhausting. They have a strong urge to learn, and find out, greater details about our universe.

They shouldn't be able to indulge in anything they don't like. When they take part in things they do not like they feel that they're not honest about themselves. Empaths are often categorized as lazy due to their refusal to be a part of something with which they don't like, and the majority of things are viewed as that.

The need to be lonely. It is essential for them to be by themselves, and that's true for children who are empath.

They are passionate about wildlife and nature. Empaths are passionate about life and in nature. They usually are pet owners in the house. They believe that animals and plants are aware of their thoughts and feelings.

They are in constant contact with the spirit world and common for them, like experiencing ghosts, spirits and ghosts. They also have access to information that scientists could struggle for years to attain. Empaths for instance were the first to realize that the universe was round, while the rest of us believed that it was flat.

They're still exhausted; they are constantly exhausted and exhausted, due to the fact that they are so susceptible to the influence of other people. This fatigue is so intense that they are unable to recover from sleep. Empaths may be diagnosed with Myalgic Encyphalomyelitis (ME). They suffer from back problems and stomach issues. The abdomen's middle is where the the solar plexus is located. In this region, empaths are sensitive to the emotions of others, which makes them weaker and could cause Irritated bowel syndrome stomach ulcers, lower back issues. The empath who doesn't appreciate their gifts may be suffering from the physical problems. They are able to catch illnesses quickly. the physical symptoms of the people close to them develop into an empath. They also infect joints and body parts from colds, eye infections, as well as the aches and pains. They often feel pains of compassion when they're near to other people.

Empaths are listening board. Empaths work together to release their burdens, and sometimes end up being their own. They feel the feelings of others and carry their feelings onto. They are able to discern the emotions of people who are close and far away, or both. The more skilled empath recognizes when someone feels unwell about themselves.

They can spot falsehoods. The empath is aware when someone isn't telling the truth. It is also evident the moment someone feels or thinks in one way, but says that they are aware of something else. To recognize that they're lying, they don't have to hear the tone of someone's voice or observe their facial expressions. They are able to intuitively discern whether or not they're lying.

It is difficult for them to watch any kind of violence. Also, they don't find information articles about the topic in papers or magazines. As a consequence empaths have a difficult time to sit in front of a television screen or read magazines and newspapers.

Sometimes they can be confused in public spaces. It is challenging for an empath to live in places like shops or stadiums as well as shopping centers with many people due to of the volume of energy released from the crowds. Their environment is planned and planned in accordance with their sensitivity. To ensure that they do not face uncomfortable, unpredictably situations that can be challenging their work schedules and responsibilities are arranged.

They are able to access cutting-edge knowledge. Empaths are tuned to knowledge They know things without having to say that they do. It's not intuition or intuition The awareness they have comes from a larger impactful source. The more powerful this gift gets, the more they're in tune with their gifts.

They can influence the mood of people. They're extremely charismatic and their energy attracts people. They begin talking and acting exactly like their counterparts when they are too busy with other people.

They are awestruck by the water. They love the energy that the oceans provide, oceans, the rivers.

The truth is that they've always been told they're too fragile and emotional. Their ability to detect emotional and physical signs isn't innate for everyone other than them, but it is theirs.

They are not tolerant of pain and when they need to take care of even the smallest injury, they are difficult to receive injections without feeling sick. They could also be advised by medical professionals that they complain too often.

They are very attentive in understanding facial expressions and body language. They are exceptionally skilled.

They are drawn by the healing professions. Nurses doctors, veterinarians, or physicians have empathy as well. Empaths are attracted by the possibility of becoming counselors human-centered workers and communicators for animals as well as teachers and caregivers.

Empaths are attracted to the healing and complementary artslike organic food, hypnotherapy psychotherapy, holistic methods such as energy, Reiki as well as psychic reading. They have a philosophical inclination in meditation, prayer yoga, and positive affirmations.

They are non-conformists who wish to be free from the limitations of the standard of living in society. A family and children. They are passionate about travel as well as freedom and adventure. Empaths are independent They do not enjoy stagnation. Rules, routines or power are things they do not like. Empaths love being able to do what they want to do at any time they wish to. They feel confined and shackled in the event that they are not able to perform their duties.

Chapter 4: The Sensitive Disorder

Do you detect or notice an elegant scent or sound that don't bother people in your vicinity? Do you often get accused of being emotionally arousing? If these traits are a reflection of your personality, then you're likely to be classified as a sensitive person (HSP). Many people mistake sensitive people as fragile, but they have qualities that they have.

According to the definition, for the term "sensitive" to refer to sensitive, it means that you are more sensitive to situations than a typical person. Let me explain. This implies that you are able to process positive and negative events more thoroughly. A person with an HSP can be overwhelmed by stimuli, such as excessive noise, high-pressure situations, and crowds.

In the opinion of According to 1. Aron the author also as the editor of the group of people with sensitivity between 20 and twenty constitutes an entire world population. In addition, high sensitivity is an innate trait meaning that they may have been raised with it. The typical HSP person is typically an introvert , extrovert or in between.

The signs of a sensitive person

It's a fact that everyone is afraid of violence. In the case of the most part, an HSP watching or hearing about violence can be a bit disturbing when you are unable to go to a movie that is scary or gory one without being affected or triggering physical ailments. A sensitive person can't take information that is based on brutality or cruelty to animals.

Tired of absorbing the emotions of other people

A person who is sensitive can be a sponge for the emotions of others, just as empathy might. It is common for someone who is sensitive to move around the room and then immediately record the moods of the individuals in it. People who are sensitive are always aware of the subtleties in communication, particularly the voice tone and the visual language. By the course of a day, one who is sensitive will experience frequently from emotional exhaustion than the rest of us.

Time pressure rattling you

There are times when you're overwhelmed with the tasks on your list to accomplish and there's not enough moment to finish it. The pressure can be a problem during your speed test in class. This typically accompanied by anxiety, and ultimately causes the student to not perform as well as he normally should. People who are sensitive are usually sensitive to stimuli and pressure.

SEPARATION

A HSP may find himself retreating to a peaceful, quiet area like a darkened room to reduce the level of stimulation and calm your nerves. This is common for someone who is an introvert or an extrovert who needs time to reflect and is at ease with his regular thoughts while in solitude.

Being jumpy

It can happen when someone sneaks onto you. Your reactions are likely to be in a state of confusion throughout the exchange. It's even more alarming to realize that an HSP has a high Moro reflex. The primary reason is that even when in non-threatening situations the nervous system of their patients is at a high level of alert.

OVERTHINKING

One thing that differentiates an HSP from the rest of us is their capacity to absorb information in a deep manner. The person is more prone to negative overthinking. If he continues to think about and over, it triggers the thoughts of anxiety.

Afraid of a loud crash

This happens when an HSP can't withstand the sound of. A car sound that is loud at your door could make you shake and disrupt your peace.

CLOTHING

This refers to being aware of the clothes you've been wearing. A scuffy fabric or restricting clothes like tight pants could cause irritation. If you are a pure HSP person is likely to take care to select their clothes carefully and avoid items that belong to specific classes. If an HSP is able to wear clothing that isn't of their preference, the entire event could result in complete discomfort.

INQUISITIVE

Hsps are always seeking answers to the most important questions about life. They'll always want to understand why certain things are happening in a certain sequence, while trying to find answers. As an HSP, you'll be wondering what the reason why certain mysteries of the universe or the nature of things don't bother others since you are.

More tolerance to pain

If it's related to discomfort of any kind such as headaches, injuries and other bodyaches, hsps tend to be more sensitive than other hsps.

Resistance to against change

The HSPs are usually comfortable with routines. The reason for this is that something new is less stimulant than something that is familiar. In the same way, an HSP is unable to taking on any negative or positive changes.

An ideal example of this is the time an HSP is offered a replacement job or is paired with the replacement candidate; they are equally overwhelmed. It's a fact that an HSP will require more time to align to the changes.

The present and alive inside world

Because you are always absorbing your thoughts creates a luxurious inner space. In your youth, you'll probably have had imaginary friends or even daydreamed without difficulty. When you reach adulthood, you'll experience more realistic dreams.

Never understood correctly

The public has repeatedly mischaracterized sensitive people. They usually believe that there's something wrong with you, while describing you by unfamiliar words like anxious, shy, or awkward. Additionally, people often label many individuals who are introverts, since they share certain characteristics like the need for more relaxation. It's a reality that approximately 30% of all hsps are introverts.

Refusing to accept a new surroundings

Sometimes your unique situation becomes your undoing. There isn't much excitement you settle in a new place or perhaps traveling to different destinations. It's due to the fact that your mind is overwhelmed with fresh stimuli.

It is easy to lose temper

It is easy to upset an HSP and make them angry just by mentioning a small issue. They are also sensitive to fluctuations the blood sugar level and they are hungry fast, especially when their stomachs are empty for a brief period of time.

STIMULLANTS

There is a group of hsps which are highly sensitive to stimulants, such as caffeine. They'll just need a small amount or a smudge to experience its effects. The other groups of hsps are vulnerable to the effects of alcohol, so they should stay clear of the use of alcohol.

Avoids conflicts

An HSP is extremely sensitive every time there's a dispute within her intimate relationship. The problem can get worse until an HSP becomes physically ill. In order to alleviate the issue, sensitive people stay clear of conflicts and will say everything to keep the other person content. This is a way to reduce tension and removing hurts.

Refuses the criticism

Every word you speak is crucial in the eyes of an HSP. The words you use can cause them to sink to the bottom. Positive words provide them with an edge and allow their power to rise. Critique can be a dagger. The sensitive people do not like negativity as it can hinder their work.

Trying to be mindful

At work or at school, people who are sensitive try not to make mistakes. Always try your best, and you're always close to perfect.

Attracted by the beauty

An HSP likes strong smells exquisite food, stunning artworks and melodies that make a huge impression on people. Certain music sounds could put into a trance-like state. It's possible that you don't have a any reason to know why some people are more sensitive to beauty than you are.

Perceptive

The person who is sensitive tends to be sensitive and observant because they can spot things quickly that others overlook. When you are a child, people generally rate you as smarter than your age.

Types of sensitive people

There are three kinds of people who are sensitive:

Feeling unsure about oneself

Be sensitive to the opinions of other people

The ability to be sensitive about one's surroundings

The Self-Sensitivity of Oneself

In this group, people are characterized by the following traits:

They tend to hold onto negative emotions and thoughts for quite a long time .

If something isn't right throughout the day, this HSP is often afflicted with physical symptoms such as headaches or anxiety.

A bad day could affect his sleeping or eating habits. He might eat less and be feel sleepy.

The person with this type of personality is always prone to tension and anxiety.

The individual is suffering from stress that he has caused himself when he is unable to meet his expectations.

The HSP is always rejected. Always irritated by small things.

The HSP performs self-comparisons, especially when it comes to physical work, financial and interpersonal. The person will feel uneasy due to unfavorable social interactions.

There's a feeling of discontent over events in the world that seem unfair or unjust.

Sensitivity to Other People

The following are the ideal way to describe this type of classification:

He often worries about what people think about him.

This type of HSP can lead to taking things personal.

The HSP type finds it difficult to forgive people, particularly when they are hurt by others .

Are squeamish at the actions of other people.

He keeps negative thoughts to himself thinking it's embarrassing to reveal them to anyone. He prefers to hide his feelings of depression rather than talk about them.

He refuses to accept criticism even though it was fair and constructively given.

He generally considers others to be an expert even when there is any evidence to support it.

This kind of HSP can overreact to serious or minor annoyances.

He is uncomfortable in groups and will find it difficult to be himself.

He's self-conscious about a couple of romantically intimate relationships. He frets about his partner's approval, and may have a naive be afraid of being rejected by his person he is with.

Sensitivity to One's Environment

The people in this category will display the following traits:

If too many things are occurring at the same time, this HSP can feel uneasy. It's apparent, especially in the crowd or in the course of a room filled with people.

It is irritable when exposed to loud noises, powerful scents or bright light sources.

is usually upset while watching a scary film or reading negative news in the media.

He may feel uneasy when he follows posts of other people on social media.

What Do You Think It Means If You're Tested as sensitive?

If you prove to that you are an HSP by conducting a test to determine if you are a sensitive person, it indicates that you have an inherited characteristic. This also means that you're portion of between 15% and 20 percent people.

A person who is sensitive reacts more strongly to events more than a normal person might do. Their brains be able to process both negative and positive information more thoroughly. This means that external stimuli like intense noises and stressful situations can cause them to become overwhelmed. The ability to be sensitive is your strongest assets. It's a huge gift, but it's not always simple to manage. For a good example, let's look at the life of Gandhi. Many people believe that he was an HSP and spent some time in prison. He was aware of how religious conflict have affected his hopes, however his leadership was a source of inspiration for others. Mahatma left a remarkable legacy of peace after he secured the freedom of India without launching war.

Tips that help an HSP in tackling concerns about stimulations

The most essential step is to recognize those situations that make you feel overwhelmed. Once you've identified the triggers you'll find ways to cut back the excessive stimulation. Utilize cognitive therapy techniques to assist you in checking the emotional responses. The next step is to do it in the case of hypersensitivity:

Respect your sensitivity. Select situations that are tolerant of your personality.

Reconsider your actions. If you are reacting to an event, take a step back, rethink the situation and stop to reflect.

Avoid external stimulation by avoiding trying to do things that you might not manage well.

Make use of the noise-canceling headphones to control the volume of sound.

When parties are held, always return to an empty space for every 30 minutes to rest.

Adjust the settings on your TV to equalize the volume of the demolition and the.

When you feel stressed, opt for breathing exercises. Exhale slowly in a slow, steady way for 3 to 5 .

Avoid stimulants like caffeine or nicotine.

Check that you've had enough rest before you face a situation that is highly stimulating.

Prayer and meditation are another form of relaxation to increase your ability to tackle your daily struggles.

Genes that cause you to be an affluent Person

There is evidence in a variety of studies that an individual who is sensitive might be a healthy, normal being. The same is certain advantages in evolution. The ability to sense is also an inheritance, but it isn't a result of one gene. The traits of personality are the result of an array of genes that make up a single. In this scenario, three distinct genes are involved in a particular. Amazingly, each one of the three genes has an impact on the nervous system and brain.

Let's look at these genes that lead you to be an incredibly sensitive person.

The Gene 'Sensitive' (Serotonin Transporter)

Serotonin is a key chemical that is found in your body and plays a variety of roles, including stabilizing your mood. However, serotonin transporter can be a substance that assists to move serotonin from the body. It's essential to balance mood in the context of private.

People who are sensitive require an individual variant of the gene for serotonin transporter which behaves in a different way. It is possible that you've this genetic variant that suggests that you have lower levels of serotonin which means you'll be more sensitive.

The gene variant isn't responsible for mood disorders on its own however it causes you to be aware of your surroundings. So you'll learn to recognize the personality that surrounds you and learn a lot from it. This kind of gene is essential for the development of children. If you associate this gene in a negative child's environment, you decrease the risk of developing depression and other illnesses throughout your life.

On the other hand, if you mix a similar gene with a safe environment, you'll see excellent outcomes when you're an adult.

The gene increases the outcomes of a good and bad childhood. For a person who is sensitive, your experiences from childhood will have more of an influence on your life later on in life. In addition, there's a chance that you can use to help you to rectify the effects of your difficult childhood. The best part is that it won't have an impact on you in the same way as it affects other people.

The Dopamine Genes

Dopamine is a brain reward chemical. There is a link between the sensitivity of the brain and 10 gene variants linked with dopamine. If you are a beginner, someone with an afflicted system might want to be less rewarded by external stimuli. It is also sense people who are vulnerable want to be to be rewarded more through positive emotional and social indicators.

If you're sensitive, you may find it difficult to accept an entire group of people to go to a noisy and crazy atmosphere and can tolerate it. If this happens, it's because your brain does not get the same dopamine rush from these loud external stimuli. This could be due to genes that are at working.

The Gene for 'Emotional Vibration'

Each person will experience life more vividly , particularly in emotionally charged times. The intensity of the experience varies across different groups of people. The high sensitivity is an immediate connection with the genetic variant that regulates it.

The emotional vividness gene has the strongest link to norepinephrine. The transmitter for norepinephrine aids in the body's stress response. It's interesting to note that there's a variation that is commonly found in hsps, which turns the dial of emotional vividness. If you are convinced that you have it, your experiences within the mental aspects of our world will be more vibrant. This means you'll be able to experience more brain activity within the areas of your brain that create profound emotional experiences as well as your own experience.

The people who are sensitive are constantly aware that they require greater emotional responses than a normal person. They'll be more likely to be aware of emotional undercurrents that make people tend to avoid anything. When you're an HSP,, you've been blessed with a wider range of emotional hues because of this genetic variant. In addition, it directs the amount of empathy and the awareness you'll be able to feel about the feelings of others.

The Benefits of Being sensitive

The Feeling of Positive Emotion Intensely

An HSP is more upset and more frequently than other people. If something honest happens, the hsps can feel satisfaction and be awed by others. A simple compliment can transform his day or last all week. In some instances, an event that is unusual occurs, which can cause a positive feelings throughout the entire month.

Enjoying Art and wonder

Hsps are ideal for aesthetes. They appreciate and are sensitive to beauty and. The HSP is often influenced by a musical or film and thus the nature of the universe. This includes watching sunrise and sunset.

They are Empathic

It's the ability to be able to see the world from the shoes of another. Studies show that HSP has more powerful empaths that are more effective than normal people. Hsps don't just feel empathy and feel compassion, but they can feel other people's emotions as though they are their own. It can also be a positive force that motivates HSP to aid people who might be in a awkward situation. The insight is that empathy is the driving force for all HSPs.

DETAIL-ORIENTED

An HSP's brain HSP can be more efficient in processing information than the average person. He is able to sift through an sign that others wouldn't and then use it to gain more understanding. This capability allows the HSPs excel when working on projects that require focus on the details which makes them diligent and skilled throughout their professional experiences.

Insanely Creative

Are you aware that sensitivity is a catalyst for imagination? If an HSP is feeling extremely emotional, he'll seek out outlets to express his own feelings. They'll go to the point of writing about their feelings or perhaps composing a little of music. This can lead to innovation and growth in their lives.

Fast Learners, Deep Thinkers

Highly sensitive people process materials more deeply. The brain of someone who is sensitive can draw connections from experiences and utilize them as an alternative solution. They require long-term memory. Long-term memory refers to it being long-term that deals with understanding and other knowledge based on concepts.

An HSP also has the capacity to absorb new information without thinking. This means they have solutions to all kinds of problems, that are a huge benefit to their job.

Chapter 5: Benefits And The Challenges Of Being An Empath

What is it that means to Be Empathic?

Attunement for an empath is an automatic response. Empaths live their everyday lives, absorbing and processing their emotions as if they were magnets. Due to this, empaths require a deliberate self-care plan and a deliberate approach to managing their emotions in order to stay clear of overwhelm (which is the result of exposure to too many stimuli) as well as anxiety and depression.

Although a strong empathic disposition is a wonderful gift however, constant exposure to other emotional reactions can result in exhaustion, depletion and feelings of unbalance. So, being able to manage your daily experience and interactions in a healthy way is essential. By using mindfulness techniques and techniques in this book empathy can help them maintain their health and alleviate the anxiety that is a constant companion wherever they travel.

The Similarities and Differences Between Empaths and Introverts

Introverts and empaths are alike with respect to many aspects, however there are some subtle differences between them. For example, both empaths as well as introverts need time to themselves to replenish their energy and find a feeling of calm towards the close of their day. The main distinction in empaths is the fact that an empath utilizes this time alone to release the tension generated by other people during the day. However, introverts require to recharge but don't necessarily have to deal with the emotions that others have triggered. There is a common misconception to assume that everyone empath is introverted. Although most empaths are introverted there are many extroverts and even ambiversal empaths that all recharge differently.

The true magic happens for empaths, regardless of whether they are extrovert or introvert when they are able to harness their unique empathic personality, enhance their strengths as empaths and then combine these strengths with the ability to process emotions to achieve a balanced equilibrium that allows them to flourish. Empaths can make difficult experiences have meaning through engaging in transformative ways to reduce anxiety and managing their emotional wellbeing.

Empath Children

Children are adept at tuning in and they learn to manage their own emotional terrain by watching their parents. Infants naturally set their heartbeat to coincide with their mother's as they nurse or cuddling or sleeping. By aligning their heartbeats, children grow and develop through a connection with their caregivers to meet their demands for food, sleep and affection. In the same way, they attune with their adult caregivers to meet their emotional requirements. As they become more attuned to their caregivers, their personality emerges. In the event that the person who is caring for them is disengaged or distant the infant may display emotions of anxiety and distress while trying to get attuned due to their need to build a relationship that they feel secure. When a baby has an active parent who is connected to their feelings and is mentally present is more likely that the child will develop an emotional bond that is secure.

Empathic children aren't any different in their need to be connected to their caregiver however, they may require less stimulation to keep the balance of their emotions. The bright lights and loud conversations, or chaotic family structures are all stimulating for a lot of children. For those who are sensitive the stimulation may be overwhelming the need for them to be connected to their parent for emotional security will be evident. Although all infants depend on their caregivers for calming their unstable moods, sensitive children may need the comfort of their parents more frequently because they are in frequent states of excessive stimulation. In addition extremely sensitive and empathic kids may exhibit an over-reactive response to stimulation when as compared with other kids.

Self-soothing is a crucial ability that children who are empathic need to manage the stress of daily life as well as sensory overload and emotional stress. An adult caregiver can assist an emotionally sensitive child by observe how the child displays self-soothing behaviours and encouraging the child to create routines that encourage these behavior. Furthermore caregivers can offer support by being a calm presence when a child is overwhelmed and exhibits emotions. They can utilize calm breathing to calm a stressed child. The act of helping a child calm down sets the basis for the child's capacity to self-soothe.

Empath Parents

Being able to feel a great amount of empathy for our children, while also helping them manage difficult emotions is an integral part of parenting. Parents who are emotionally empathetic must manage their own feelings while observing the emotional state that their kids are experiencing. The ability to establish and maintain proper boundaries is essential to performing the emotional work that helps the entire family. Parents who are emotionally connected will be able to feel their children's emotional needs however it doesn't need to come in the way of their wellbeing. It's essential to find ways to soothe yourself as well as practice self-care and learn to maintain a healthy emotional routine to build a solid foundation of harmony within the family. Be aware that children connect to their caregivers, and are looking at them in order to feel and to develop an emotional vocabulary. Being attentive to your emotional health as an empath will help your children to follow suit and enhance their emotional ability.

A parent who empathizes has an abundance of emotional resources available to the family. For instance An Animal Empath can teach children how to show compassion towards animals and create an ongoing relationship of love for animals and the satisfaction from this care. The Intuitive Empath is able to use the five senses to present the world of wonder and curiosity for their children, and also help to develop their own senses. Parents who are Empaths can use their empathy to determine what they will do to spend moments with their kids. For example, artistic Empaths could visit a museum with their children and bond with their children through the shared sensory experience of observing an artwork. In the same way, Physical Empaths are able to connect with their children through yoga, sports or other physical exercises.

Parents want to be thought of as the perfect caregivers who are able to help their children navigate their challenges in a gentle manner. Parents are often insecure about their parenting abilities most of the time because they aren't sure whether the decisions they're making are the right ones or not. They're not trying their best.

Being a parent is a challenge. However, the desire for an unending affection and love is what drives people to seek out parents at all. However, for all the wonderful bonding that oxytocin and parents share with their children There are also moments of frustration, exhaustion and deep depletion of their souls. Children are noisy and messy, they are also costly, and sometimes endless. They have the capacity to shake an empath to their very core.

In addition, the way that surrounds raising kids is more demanding today than it ever been. Choices regarding daycare, spirituality education, as well as expectations about food can make parents feel judged and slighted. Using empathy to help improve parenting skills is an effective instrument for self-help and direction that is embraced by the groups that comprise the ideal "village" that we must make beautiful, well-integrated human beings.

RED As an emotional empath It is possible to determine which emotions are yours as well as those belonging to someone else by asking yourself two questions.

The first step is to ask, "What was I feeling at the time I felt angry (or emotional or sad)?" Third, "Was there a triggering incident that triggered this feeling?" If you're feeling good but there was no obvious trigger, it's likely that you were able to pick up another's emotions. Relax and let the feelings go by taking several deep breaths in order to calm yourself.

As an INDIGO Animal Empath, it is clear the fact that all animals possess their own own ways of communicating, and some animals do not are interested in touching.

It's easy to sense that a dog is anxious, fearful or frightened. Communicate these signals to children so that they can develop a trusting connection with animals. For instance, if the dog's tail is down and its lips curled, it's best to watch the dog from a distance. Your child's motive for wanting to play with animals may be to get a cuddle. However, it is possible for things to become harmful for both children and animals in the event that the complicated behavior of animals are not taken into consideration. Your closeness to animals is something you should teach your children and help them become aware of these subtle cues.

VIOLET As an intuitive empath You have a monopoly on the sensory information that you receive.

You've seen how to talk yourself off of the things you've learned and don't be a believer in your instincts. Think of a time you questioned your intuition and the negative repercussions that resulted. Record the event and then focus on the way you feel within your body. Note any emotions that come up. Journaling about the experience will give it meaning and strengthens your understanding of emotions. Keep this journal entry as a reference point and use it anytime you're being unsure of your abilities as parents.

Empathy: How to Develop It?

Certain people are more empathetic than others, and some have less But the good thing is the fact that empathy could be built and developed and strengthened. How?

The most important stage is being humble. This does not necessarily mean that you should be slack or underestimate your talents and abilities however, it is about being curious and open to people and what they do and think. This attitude of mind and attitude is the basis of active listening. This can be one of the key elements to understanding.

Also, you need to be able to be aware of your emotions and emotions. Knowing your moods and how to manage them will allow you to be able to communicate with people with a clear mind, without "gut" judgments and be able to act in a respectful and balanced manner. To be able to understand people and connect with the people around you, you need to develop self-awareness.

Another option is to leave the comfort zones and connect with those who don't belong to your typical circle of friends and acquaintances. The ability to open yourself to other and unfamiliar realities completely different from your normal day and life experiences can help you get valuable experiences and create new acquaintances. It also increases your self-awareness , and ultimately your ability to comprehend, read and relate to the feelings of others.

Chapter 6: The Dark Side Of Empaths

The world might not be able to see the world, but you do. The empath in you very smart and well-groomed as the darkness that comes from experiencing this mysterious blessing. Anguish and pain that can be fascinating to individuals who feel every vibrating energy around them like 1,000,000 fingers were cutting your spirits.

You are the one that others often turn to to carry their load and, as a result you are seen as solid, reliable character. In fact, you're a bit sensitive and yet you seem to adjust so easily to the ferocious conflict that is forced upon you.

It isn't often that people know that inside, you're a fiery jumble of divergent thoughts, mixed together to form an unfathomable and endless rumble that you fight to silence.

Sometimes, it can be overwhelming until it appears as if an invisible hand is wrapped around your neck. It's a significant factor that is so intense that it requires every bit of your strength not to collapse.

The sudden and negative changes in energy are extreme in how they appear from nowhere and give you a chance to make plans. They strike you like a freight train leading you into a spiral of devastation, chaos and hurt.

It's actually the negative energies that you feel the most and is made worse by the things which surrounds you. The sadness, the angst and the destructive power that causes it overwhelm you more than the large-hearted, and the great can help you rise up. The world was not designed for people like you.

Within your heart, your feelings can be anywhere you are feeling them profoundly and with incredible force; there is no middle ground, and or volume knob to drain your faculties. It's both physically and physically exhausting to go the course of your life with a remarkably constant level of high-energy, but you manage... to a degree for most of the time... in order to present an ordered, though every now and then off-kilter appearance.

It could be an insular presence, as an empath. Regardless whether you're surrounded by people, the merging of energy can cause you to feel confused. You are unsure of the point at which you finish and where others begin as well as this blurring of personal boundaries only makes it harder to maintain your personal sense of being.

Unfortunately, this feeling of isolation can place you into the hands of people who attempt to take advantage of you. The desire for a persona and being accepted or loved for who you are, could cause you to fall into traps created by the controllers and victims. They are after sensitive individuals such as you, who want to feel the sense of belonging.

Being the kind and admiring person you are, do not see the dangers that lurk for the sake of what they're worth. You're not paying attention to the evil intentions of those not feeling and, in your efforts to aid them, you risk becoming involved in their games.

You'll always feel the desire to aid others It is in your habit to put your focus to the problems and needs of those who are in a challenging circumstance, since you have through one method or another way are assisting people with your help is a good idea.

You aren't aware of the burden that this level of kindness puts on your life and, when it is, resist the urge to acknowledge it due to a paranoid worry about actually being compelled by your vile forces. You prefer to walk along the streets, slouched against the burden of the world descending upon you, rather than being able to walk freely and observe the pain and suffering of your own before you.

The evasion isn't good in the long run because at times, your psyche and heart get a workout, being pushed to the edge by an inability to solve the major issues. In delaying the start by a few days, you're sunk into deeper in which you frantically throw yourself to stay away from the other world. You get rid of everything and protect yourself honestly and honestly, so that you can go deep and confront the hidden issues.

The pain you feel during this period is quite awe inspiring and how can it be to be less for someone who is confronted with feelings in an intense and profound manner? The torture you endure is on the basis that your heart is allegorically apart as you fight all the turmoil that resides there , both yours and the food you've consumed.

When it comes to hearts, you're typically not willing to surrender your entire heart to a lover who is caring that causes you to feel a bit of sadness and sorrow. But, to let your heart open completely, you'll be able to experience the totality, unbridled strength of love in its purest form. It is impossible to say whether you're able to deal with this incredible power, nor do you wonder if your accomplice has the ability to change their ways in the event that you were to allow all access.

You protect yourself with a reasonable manner and never show your entire hand. You keep some thing in the back to prevent future pain from taking your entire life. Whatever you want to happen is that you are able to embrace love in all its strength and force as you believe within your soul that this is what you truly need.

It is not a good idea to be overwhelmed by your incredible and yet challenging blessing. There is confidence... .there exists always confidence.

The dark side isn't going to be able to prevail for the rest of your life. It is possible to, with a bit of instruction, and the support of those who care for you, discover ways to cope with the piercing severity of the emotions that you feel. Your pain and sorrow could be eased and you'll be able to determine what emotions are yours and which originate from other sources of fuel.

There is no need to have your watchman constantly up There is a way to let others in without feeling overwhelmed by what you think. It is achieved through acknowledgement of your sincere effort, the unwavering determination not to let your valuable quality end up in your deep-rooted prison.

Chapter 7: How To End The Emotional Overload

Overwhelmedness is a common occurrence today because of many favorable circumstances around. There's plenty of stress be thrown around by everyone and when we mix it with personal problems anyone with a clear mind will want to let off some of their emotions. That's when a person who is compassionate can step in and help someone else.

What happens when the great Empath has experienced a fair portion of negative emotions? How can he stay out of the danger of getting lost in unresolved, unspoken emotions? Why those who are extremely sensitive are more susceptible to emotional exhaustion?

It is the nature of empaths to be able to feel the feelings of others, no matter how "bad" as it might be, which often results in the healer needing "emotional therapy." A great strategy that many empaths employ is to stop an "emotional bomb" from forming instead of combating it when it does occur. This strategy allows greater control over the events of one's life by choosing the best option instead of merely following the flow of life. Prevention can take many forms and forms, and can range from the choices made in life to small "tricks."

Awareness

One practice that has helped many empaths was awareness. It is a general concept that concentrates on the sensory perception , or our own internal state. Both are useful when you're an Empath. Being conscious of your feelings and thoughts can help highly sensitive people distinguish their personal emotions from the energy and emotions they "pick off in the streets." In addition, suppose that someone is grounded in his environment and therefore is conscious of the external stimuli. In this case it is possible to develop an easier method of absorbing the information without becoming overwhelmed.

Energy

Another idea that aids in the prevention of illness is that energy. Empaths are spiritually gifted They can sense and read energies. In addition to reading they also take advantage of the energies around them. Energy can be found in positively and negatively oriented forms. Positive energies are triggered through emotions like forgiveness, love and kindness, whereas negative ones are triggered by anger, sadness, and so on. These energies may come from people or dwell in various locations and places. Consider energy as baggage you carry around or leave. Empaths are able to carry the baggage and make it themselves, even though it's not the best choice for them. Being aware of these energy sources can help an empathic person decide which burdens to keep and which ones to let go, thus avoiding the possibility of overload.

Sometimes , the problems of others aren't solved by an outsider regardless of how much they are able to understand the issue. Empaths are inclined to take the problems of the world in their own hands and failing to find an answer can cause them to feel emotionally exhausted. Although it can be difficult for empaths to accept, it is impossible to help everyone. Individuals must be able to learn from mistakes made and learn from of them. Nothing can be as effective as hitting at the ceiling and tackling the consequences. Therefore, empaths must be able to accept their own personal experiences and not take their mistakes as personal accidents. Be a part of the solution by incorporating positive emotions and energy into the mix, and then detaching your emotions from the event.

Finding the balance

Finding the right balance could be an important factor in living a peaceful life. There's so much happening in the mind of a sensitive person that it's not difficult to slip into the depths of thoughts or emotions. Awareness is a crucial instrument to stop this balance from falling away. Everyone has their own definition of a balanced equilibrium. It's up to you to carry the obligation to discover the element that will help to unwind and distinguish those positive energies from negative ones, and to reduce the harmful "absorptions." As I said before there are some smart ways to keep you on the safer side with just some practicing. Be attentive to your reactions to various circumstances and identify the trigger.

Different strategies can help to help or completely prevent emotional overstimulation. If you want to be more specific the method on its own will bring you out of that poor mental state, but through doing it repeatedly often, it will be a beneficial method of preventing. Being aware of how you can work your energy by being aware, consciously selecting a response to an emotional experience, and balancing your life will alter your life for the better and give you strategies to be safe while trying to help others.

Empaths as well as Emotional Intelligence

Emotional intelligence refers to the ability to keep track of your mood and deal with the emotions of others. In order to be emotionally smart, you must be able be able to recognize the various emotions, and then categorize them in appropriately. After you have done this it is time to apply the knowledge you've gathered to guide your actions as well as influence the behavior of others.

EMOTIONAL Intelligence is the thing we employ when we place ourselves in others' shoes or have more deep conversation with the spouses of our children or handle a troublesome child. It lets us know our own behavior better, communicate effectively with other people, and lead a the life we want to live by making good decisions.

How to Improve Emotional Intelligence

While empaths are able to be able to understand emotions on a more profound level, it doesn't necessarily mean that they are able to manage or distinguish their emotions from other people. To enhance their capabilities in this regard, they must first enhance the level of their intelligence. This will enable them to discern their own feelings and those of others which will allow them to be able to recognize and efficiently manage these emotions. To improve emotional intelligence, you must concentrate on five essential elements in emotional intelligence.

SELF-AWARENESS. If you don't first develop your self-awareness you will not be able to create the other components needed to improve you emotional intelligence. Being aware of your emotions is vital when it comes to your ability to identify your feelings as well as how you deal with your emotions, the triggers that cause them and how their feelings affect others surrounding them. Knowing your emotions will help you differentiate between your own feelings and the ones you experience from other people.

SELF-REGULATION. Self-regulation is one of the most important factors in enhancing emotional intelligence. If you're able to regulate yourself and respond in a timely manner to your feelings. If you're those who are empaths it is an important capability to learn because it concentrates on regulating the effect your emotions can influence you and the effects of other people's emotions. One of the most effective methods for self-regulation is to concentrate upon your breath. If you are overloaded by emotion, whether your own or someone else's, it's recommended to pay attention towards your breath. Concentrate on staying at a steady, steady pace. This will enable you to let your emotions run through their course while maintaining your mind clear. As the intensity of the emotions subsides, you'll be able to recognize your strengths and the ones that are inherited from other people. Being an empath may be a beneficial and swift method to stay calm when you are confronted by overwhelming emotions from multiple individuals. Keep your attention on your breath. If you realize that you're paying too much focus on the emotions you feel and are not able to focus, you should remind yourself to go back to your breathing.

Self-regulation can make the growth in other areas in your personal emotional intelligence. By self-regulating, you will be aware of the control you have over your personal emotions. The ability to recognize empathy allows you to manage better the way you let the emotions of others affect you. If you don't build your self-control and self-control, you'll constantly feel overwhelmed and overwhelmed by emotions , and will react in unproductive or unhealthy ways.

MOTIVATION. A variety of factors can inspire people Most empaths are motivated with the need to help other people. To boost your motivational capabilities it is important to track what you've accomplished even if it did not go as you expected. If you are an empath it could be the list of ways you can help others or the number of instances you have changed the negative energy that you take in into positive. Motivation comes in various ways, but you need first acknowledge and be proud of the achievements you make. Empaths may be in a position of difficulty when faced with a tidal wave in negative energies. With this feature the majority of empaths learn to appreciate how they've overcome the negative experiences and concentrate on the positive outcomes of the day.

EMPATHY. Empathy is one of the skills that empaths don't need to develop since they're naturally empathic. This doesn't mean that there should not be any room for improvement. Empathy lets you put yourself in the other's shoes, but it's important to assist the person to process what they are feeling. This is the goal of all empaths, however this is the point where things could be out of balance when it comes to the empathy aspect. Many empaths go to the point of being overly sensitive, which can make their energy levels decrease and cause empaths to cut off their abilities to help others. Finding the balance between being able to feel the feelings of another and the most effective methods to assist is a delicate line. The best way to help empaths find a better equilibrium is to practice loving kindness. It's a straightforward process which allows you to show compassion and love to people who are in need in your life, or to people you feel grateful to. It's a wonderful practice to assist empaths to release the negative energy that they take from other people and turn it into positive and loving vibrations. It also helps you increase your compassion for other people as well, which is a different characteristic that empaths acquire.

Social skills. To develop healthy social skills may be challenging. However, if you work on this vital aspect in emotional intelligence you'll be able to utilize the other abilities you've been working on. If you improve your social abilities and develop your social skills, the ability to use your empathy gift to help others become easier to handle. Social skills are the ability to manage and sustain relationships with others as well as the influence you exert on them. How can you influence them in a more positive way to influence the relationship in a positive direction for you both? Enhancing your emotional aptitude as an empath could significantly help you distinguish your feelings from those of others and provide you with a clear understanding of how to utilize your skills to the maximum benefit. However, increasing your emotional IQ as with all things involved in your life, calls for an equilibrium. If you are focusing too much on enhancing one area of your emotional intelligence over another, you could get distracted from the goals you have set, yourself and confidence in your capabilities. In addition to enhancing their emotional intelligence, empathy may also enhance their abilities by utilizing other techniques and practices.

How Empathy Influences Your Life

I

If you're an Empath You are well-aware the extent to which your gift will affect your daily routine and your daily life. Being sensitive to a variety of aspects can affect your ability to be happy or be successful in all of your daily life situations. Empathy is generally not a debilitating condition and you're not required to be an elitist to be an Empath. It can however assist you to understand the ways that being an Empath affects your daily life.

None of these scenarios can be applied to you. As an Empath there are others who are affected by certain, or even all of these scenarios. It is beneficial that all Empaths to be aware and an understanding of the different ways that your particular sensitivities influence your overall life.

Home

It is your home where you unwind and sleep, cook your meals, relax and time with your family or just relax and host parties or visitors Explore yourself further and seek refuge. The majority of homes reflect the feelings about their souls and how they feel about themselves as individuals. We can see a myriad of places all over the world with an alternative definition that defines what "home" is actually about However, in this instance we're talking about the physical structure you visit for relaxation and comfort as well as personal enjoyment.

Your home has a lot of energy, and it fluctuates like the energy of a person. When your home is calm, peaceful and safe, warm and comfortable, then the energy of your home is in alignment with who you are and the way you feel. If your home is anxious and tense, dark or uneasy, it could be a sign that someone else's energy has affected your home as well as the way you live.

As an EMPATH You are aware of the way emotions of a person can leave an footprint, or even a residue to your energy.

There are a variety of rooms in the house Some of them may be more or more intense than others. If you're sensitive to loud sounds and bright lighting, and other people's energy, it could be difficult to be in the living room everyone else who is watching football on Friday nights or the most popular sitcom.

The KITCHEN is a lively space where there are many cooking and baking pans, quick actions to ensure that the meal is cooked within a certain timeframe, and everybody searching for a place to eat dinner simultaneously. The kitchen is also that is filled with strong aromas of noises, odors, and other aspects that can be very stimulating.

The bedroom is where you can rest and relaxation are essential and is often referred to as the heart of the home's sanctuary. If you're dealing with uncomfortable and unpleasant emotions in your bedroom due to others or issues with your relationship. If that is the situation, you won't be able to rest until you have removed and removed that negative energy from your sleep. Many Empaths experience insomnia because they hold on to their emotions and feelings from other people and take them to bed to sleep.

Work

The workplace is always changing, can take many forms and is a place where many people are involved. If you're an Empath and you are happy in your daily life, you've probably already chosen the best career for you to keep in tune with your talents and energy. Yet, many Empaths find themselves in careers or jobs which don't match their abilities and result in them feeling less than of inspired.

The most important thing to remember concerning all workplace-related events or dynamic can be that each have particular energy for the entire team you work with. It is possible that you do not feel the necessity to compete for the major job, or be your best friend with everyone in work, or fight about deadlines, but you'll need to confront the motivation that is behind these activities. Many people put a lot in pressure for themselves at the workplace. A lot of people are competitive when they the job for promotions and raises that can be an awesome satisfaction for work well-done. But, you're also being absorbed by your colleagues who are waiting for that big bonus and can be overwhelming you and drain your energy.

There is a chance of intra-office conflict between colleagues and, as an Empath working in the company you could be taking the majority of the problems with a certain person, even if you aren't in agreement with what that people say or feel about the new employee. Some people are very vocal about their boss or about the system of hierarchy in the workplace that can cause an uneasy feeling on the floor when the boss arrives. Many people feel the tension within the room or office all the time, however, the Empath experiences it five times more strongly and is required to deal with the stress of work in a different manner. If you're not grounded and balancing your energy on a regular basis and you start to behave as other employees do when dealing with the boss, even though you have never had any problems with the boss at all. The Empath is prone to feeling overwhelmed or emotional due to the ease with which it is to absorb the energy of others and begin believing it is their own.

The WORKPLACE is full of kinds of people from different backgrounds, personal stories complex home lives and unresolved emotions. There's a good chance that you have happy, grounded, content positive, professional colleagues. However, for those who are Empath it's easy to determine which negative energy you are the most at risk of.

Perhaps you haven't developed an awareness that you are able to connect your abilities to empathy to your job and this is the perfect time to begin.

Chapter 8: What Can You Tell Whether Your Empath?

Empaths are prone to be affected by the environment and possess the capacity to be aware of people around them who are able to feel and think.

Psychologists can use empath as a term to describe an individual who exhibits great empathy, frequently to the point that they take on people's discomfort at own cost. But the word "empath" could also be an occult term that describes an individual with special psychic abilities to detect the emotions and energy of others. This chapter will examine what it means to be an empath in a psychological sense.

There are many benefits of becoming an empath. The good thing is that empaths are generally excellent good friends. They are excellent listeners. They are always there to help friends in situations of the greatest need. Empaths are kind and heartfelt. Empaths are also extremely user-friendly and emotionally smart.

Certain of the incredibly good traits that make empaths amazing friends can prove challenging for the empaths. Because empaths are sensitive to the same emotions that their friends are experiencing, they could be overwhelmed by intense emotions such as anger or anxiety. Empaths are more likely to take on issues of other people with the same fervor as they do their own. It's usually hard to establish limits on their own and to refuse to say no when confronted with too much.

It is also common for empaths to feel tired when they are around other people. They are generally introverts and they require a particular amount of time alone to recharge. A study conducted in 2011 has suggested a connection between people who are highly empathic and anxiety and stress caused by social interaction. It can be overwhelming for groups to feel empathy for, as they tend to be too aware of individuals' voices and the constant conversation. People usually feel at their most at ease when at peace with the natural world.

Empaths are extremely sensitive and precisely tuned instruments when it concerns sensations. They can feel anything, often at a high level and are more prone to think about sensations. Instinct is the lens through which they perceive the world. Empaths are naturally giving spiritually attuned, spiritually attuned, and excellent listeners. If you're looking for an open heart, they've the heart you've been looking for. Through thin and thick they're available to you as world-class caretakers.

The hallmark of empaths is their ability to understand the place you're coming from. They can be able to do this without having to deal with people's emotions. But, just like me along with many of my customers some end up becoming an angst-sucking sponge for better or worse. This can be a problem when it comes to the ability to soak up positive feelings and all the beautiful things. The bodies absorb these feelings and develop if their empathies are centered around love and peace. Negativity, however, typically can be stressful, and even threatening. Therefore, they're easily spotted by emotional vampires, whose anxiety or anger can harm empathy. As a defense subliminal, they can increase their the weight of a buffer. If they're thin, they're more susceptible to negativeness. It is a way to miss the motivation behind the overindulgence. Additionally, the level of sensitivity may be frustrating when it comes to romantic relationships. Many are single, due to the fact that they've never figured out how to work out their individual cohabitation needs with when they are with a person.

Empaths absorb the emotional impact of stress they can trigger depression, anxiety attacks or a craving for food, drug and sexual cravings as well as a variety of physical symptoms that are not a traditional medical diagnosis , ranging from fatigue to anxiety. Since my personality is empathic I would like to assist all my empath patients develop the ability to feel at ease and at ease.

Empathy shouldn't cause you to feel uncomfortable constantly. Since I've been able to be in alignment with myself and avoid engaging in the societal ills Empathy continues to make me feel more free, bringing out my compassion, vitality and a sense of the amazing. To determine if you're an empath with emotion, do the following test.

You can ask yourself:

* Do I have the title of "too emotionally" or too sensitive?

If a person you know is struggling, should I feel it as well?

* Do my feelings get easily injured?

* Am I exhausted emotionally by the crowds, and needing some time to recover?

Do my nerves become upset by smells, sounds or extreme conversations?

* Should I drive my car to places in order to be able to leave whenever I want?

* Do I eat too much to cope with emotional stress?

* Do I fear getting swallowed by relationships with intimate people?

If you answered "yes" to any one of the above questions, then you're at the very least an of an empath. Responding "yes" in more than three of these questions indicates that you've found your emotional nature.

Accepting that you're an empath can be the very first stage towards being in control of your feelings instead of getting sucked into them. Being aware of your empathy can improve your self-care and strengthen relationships.

Evidence That You Are an Empath

If you're looking to learn more about what is an empath? And if you possess an innate ability to empathize Here are some characteristics and indications that you might be able to identify with.

Your compassion is built-in.

It's the ability that helps you comprehend other people's experiences and emotions beyond your own perspective.

If your friend just lost their dog that was 15 years old. Empathy allows you to feel the depth of grief she's feeling even if you've not lost a pet before.

As an empath you go beyond. You perceive and feel sensations as if they belonged to your own experiences. The joy or discomfort of someone else can become your pain or joy.

Intimacy is overwhelming.

Empaths typically encounter difficulties with frequent close contact that can cause romantic relationships to be difficult.

You want to make connections and establish a lasting connection. But, spending too much time with someone can cause anxiety, stress or worry about getting lost within the relationships.

It is possible to experience the sensation of sensory overload or "torn nerves" feeling that comes from too much talking or touching. If you attempt to express your desire to be alone to your partner, you take on their anger and are more irritable.

Establishing healthy, well-defined boundaries can ease the burden for empaths. The protection of your mental and emotional well-being is also essential for you, as otherwise the energy you have will be taken out of your body.

You've got the right intuition.

Have you ever felt that you have a an instinctive sense to believe that something isn't correct? Perhaps you sense that someone has cheated or can be good or bad in your gut? You feel empathy in this scenario.

Empaths can detect subtle clues to other people's thoughts, such as the ability to determine if someone is honest or not.

Being an empath could put a lot of trust in your intuition in making choices. While some may think you are spontaneous, the reality is that you're trusting in your own intuition to guide you to the best choice for you.

You enjoy nature.

Anyone can benefit by being in the natural surroundings. Empaths may feel more attracted to nature and even remote areas, since natural spaces provide a relaxing area to relax from the tense emotions, sounds, and emotional states.

It is possible to feel at peace while hiking in a sunny forest or watching waves crash on the shore. A peaceful stroll through a green space or a long time in the shade of trees can bring you back to your senses, reduce anxiety, and assist you unwind.

It is difficult to thrive in crowds.

According to research empaths may absorb positive or negative energy just being in someone's company. When there is a lot of activity or a crowd this sensitivity may be increased until it is nearly unbearable.

Empaths are more sensitive to everything in comparison to a normal person. If you are able to quickly discern the emotions of others and feel, you're likely to struggle to deal with emotions "sound" of an audience, or even an enumeration of fewer individuals, for a prolonged duration.

If you're picking up negative emotions, feelings, or even physical discomfort from the people around you You may feel overwhelmed or physically sick. In the end, you might be inclined to be alone or limit your company to just a few.

There is no reason to worry.

Empaths do not simply feel for someone else, they feel for someone. Being able to feel the feelings of others in such a profound way can make you feel the need to take action for them. Empaths are obligated to assist with any manner. When an empath is unable to help another person, they feel dissatisfied.

Empaths are unable to be happy when someone else suffering or struggling. Therefore, they will take advantage of the natural instinct to help in alleviating their suffering even if it means being the one to take it in.

Be concerned about other people's well-being isn't bad however it can cause you to neglect your personal requirements. Involvement with others may result in fatigue and burnout Therefore, it is essential to keep some energy in reserve.

People can easily trust you.

People who are compassionate, sensitive and sensitive are great listeners. Others, particularly those you love dearly, could feel at ease with your help and turn to you first when they encounter difficulties or have issues.

Due to a lot of concern to others and their feelings, people who empathize experience difficulties recognizing when they're in danger of becoming overwhelmed. So, finding the right equilibrium is crucial. In the absence of limits, uncontrolled generosity and sensibility can create the conditions to "emotion dumps" which may be too much for you to handle in any time.

Due to the fact that they trust, empathy are susceptible to manipulation, ploys or manipulation. Your desire to help people in need can make you blind to signs of evil or malice.

If you feel pain, it is important to recognize the discomfort that comes from habits and want to help. However, it's not always your decision to decide if someone else does not want your help.

You're more sensitive to smells, noises or sensations.

The oversensitivity of an empath does not just relate to his feelings. It's not easy to differentiate between empaths and hypersensitive people, but you might find that empaths are less sensitive to what's happening around them.

The signs could comprise:

Fragrance and smells can have a greater impact on you.

The physical and sound of jarring can affect you more strongly.

You can choose to listen to audio or video at low volumes , or gain information through reading.

Certain sounds can cause an emotional reaction.

You need the time to recharge.

People who are oversensitive can easily be exhausted and fatigued by their exposure to other people's difficulties and pains. A flurry of positive feelings can wear you out, which is why it's vital to take the time required to get your mind back on track.

If you don't protect yourself from negative thoughts You will probably get exhausted, which could negatively impact your health and well-being.

Being a solo person doesn't mean the person is introverted. Empaths can also be extroverts, or even fall somewhere across the spectrum. Some people can enthrall youuntil you reach that level of overwhelm.

Extroverted empaths could require more attention to find the perfect equilibrium between spending time with other people and replenishing the emotional reserve of their.

You don't like conflicts.

You're likely to fear or avoid conflict when the person you are empath.

People who are not caring can cause harm to oversensitive people. Any slight criticism, deliberate or not, can cause a heartache to an empath.

Arguments and fights can also create more stress, considering that you're not only focusing on your emotions and reactions. Additionally, you're absorbing the emotions of others. If you're trying to be attentive to everyone's suffering don't be able to comprehend the way that even minor disagreements could be difficult to handle.

You're always the odd guy out.

Despite being extremely attuned to other's feelings many empaths find it difficult to relate to people.

People may not comprehend why you feel exhausted and anxious at the same time. It is possible that you are unable to comprehend the emotions and feelings that you experience or feel as if you're distinct from others, leading to an empath that keeps to him. You may avoid talking about your sensitive feelings and share your feelings, which makes you don't feel off from the crowd.

The world needs to be aware that it's never easy to feel like you are not a part of the community and yet you feel a deep concern for other people. The empath is a unique present for the entire world. It's rare, sure yet it's an essential aspect of your persona.

You are usually alone.

It is the sanctuary for empaths for him to recover from the tense and uncomfortable emotions. However, being away for too long could cause harm to the empath's mental health. There are many kinds types of solitude, some could offer more therapeutic benefits than others.

Take time to be in nature whenever you can and meditate in a peaceful park, take a walk through the rain, go for an idyllic drive, or even a stroll in the garden.

You should think about adding an animal into your daily routine if you find that people take a lot out of you. Empaths may connect with animals more deeply and gain the deepest comfort from this bond.

It is difficult to draw boundaries.

Boundaries are important in every relationship.

If you're an empath you might find it difficult to turn off your ability to feel. You may also struggle to stop giving even when you're not feeling any energy left. If the opposite is true you might believe that limits indicate that you don't really care about your loved ones.

Borders become more important because other people's experiences have such a huge influence on empathy. They allow you to set limits regarding actions or words that could negatively impact your feelings, allowing you to fulfill your desires.

If you are unable to be able to distinguish your emotions from those around you Perhaps it's time to think about establishing a healthy boundary with the help of a psychotherapist.

Your perspective is different.

Your intuition and your emotions influence you and you're more likely to notice aspects about others or connect with them in a way others aren't able to.

However, this connection to other people can come with a disadvantages. Cultures that restrict open emotional communication may limit creativity and efficiency and cause the empath to be disengaged, disengaged and undeveloped.

Sometimes, it is difficult to manage your emotional and sensory overloaded.

Empaths can have a difficult time securing their feelings.

Healthy boundaries and self-care habits can protect yourself, particularly from negative emotions and negative energy. Emotional "sound" around you can cause serious anxiety if you don't have the skills to deal with it.

Perhaps you're having a hard to manage overstimulation on your self, which is affecting your daily life and preventing your from relationships or other goals you have for yourself. If this is the scenario, a counselor can help you establish boundaries and discover self-care strategies.

Keep in mind that your feelings and needs are as important as those that you observe in the people around you.

Chapter 9: Signs That You Might Be Psychic And The Describe The Exercise To Learn About It

There is a sense that something awful is about to take place before it happens.

You can forecast the future.

There are ghostly figures as well as other non-human beings.

It is when you know that you are thinking about someone else or is talking about you, but has no way to know the details (other that through the medium of telepathy).

Your dreams are extremely detailed and vivid, but not scary or weird.

Your dreams become reality (this isn't often however, it can happen).

Some people may think that your thoughts are different from theirs and the reverse is true, you could complete sentences with each other and think in the mind of someone else and look up reviews from afar without attempting to do it in a deliberate manner, etc...

You already know the gender of a baby who is not yet born.

You can easily gauge what someone's feeling even if they are on the phone.

Each of these is a sign of ESP. Some require more research to understand what's going on, however that's an element of fun...learning about your own personality and the things that make you unique and distinctive.

Remember that if you are gifted with intuition, these typically manifest when you're young. It doesn't matter if you were born on the astral plane or not. when psychic abilities manifest through your day-to-day life they'll be genuine and authentic...they are not fake.

They aren't something that you could learn in a weekend course to apply against you. They are natural abilities that are in your soul since birth...if they were birthed on the astralplane, your psychic abilities are more intense, but they will remain.

If you've never developed psychic abilities, it doesn't mean that you're not an telepath. The reason behind this is straightforward, it requires both clairaudience and telepathy, or the capability to hear without having an outside source of listening to it, in order to communicate with distant people.

If you've never had these traits, you could maintain a strong connection to the spirit world, or even be an angel.

It's okay to experiment and discover new talents that result from an Astral Projection or are a natural psychic gifts.

Astral is everywhere around us in every thought and emotion with every thought and action within every dream or dream... We are in a realm with duality (light/dark) that is far beyond the realm of our everyday life... Astral is the place where our thoughts and emotions leave us when we are not. We are accountable for our actions in this world, whether they are good or not.

Astral projection isn't about searching for negative energy or entities. Instead, it's about communicating.

Through exploring the astral realm it is possible to connect with loved ones who passed away and continue to play an important role of their life.

We may also connect with others who share similar interests to ours or discover those we aren't yet aware or perhaps have a reason for.

As you will observe from the following stories numerous people have experienced profound and positive experiences with spirits of animals in their astral manifestation.

Here is a collection of her personal astral experiences with animals which she outlined in "Nightside the Gnosis" (page 116-117):

"... I'm not speaking of an animal, cat, rats or anything else normal... instead, I am speaking of a fish such as the catfish or sturgeon that is considered to be an "superior" spirits... When I was 14 years old older, I vividly imagined seeing the image of an unidentified woman. As per the psychic powers I possess... I recognized that these features were familiar, but I did not identify the person until much later. Mrs. Charles Borden (a white woman, who was around my age) was from Basking Ridge, New Jersey. She passed away in the 1920s. When I first met her, she shared with me a number of ghostly experiences. But none were as mysterious as the astral vision she experienced during the beginning of my psychic exploration... It is unclear if this was due to my emotional and mental state at that time or if it was because I had some connection with her after she died due to an experience prior to death I'm not sure. However, it did happen:

It's quite unique the number of people who have had their adventures in the astral realm with animals while traveling within the "astral bodies." The stories are so precise that they could be from someone who is very knowledgeable about the animal in question.

Here's an example I believe originates directly from Bill Chalker. Please keep in your mind that these aren't my personal experiences. Moreover, the quote is to educate the public!

"On my very first projection in the countryside I came across the dog who chased me before disappearing. When I was in my second projection, I got chased by an animal. It was a terrier type dog with black and white markings and brownish-gray on the lips. It's eyes were dull and smelled foul. While I was asleep it began to pursue me , and then growl. I tried to escape but realized that I was in my body. After a few minutes I decided to repay the compliment (this can be done in the event of a good effort) and began chasing the dog. The dog ran for a few miles before disappearing... When I was in my 3rd astral projection the first thing I saw was that I saw a large dog running towards me on an unpaved road. Its coloring was pinkish-gray with brown markings on its eyes. Its teeth were huge and sparkled when it opened the mouth. It was furious at me. ..."

Here are some of the quotes of Philip K. Dick's book, "The Exegesis" (page 14):

"I have two ways of getting out of my body. One method is to approximate as close as possible the random vibrations of sound around me before fading away to the backdrop... Another technique can be to make a negative cut the air. When I place my hands on my eyes, I could force a particular portion of the surrounding vibration to the opposite side and give them an area to focus. This creates a space between them, which helps me to disappear. The analogy is similar to describing a face in general terms, so that you are able to clearly observe his nose, and then telling him, "Yes, but look at the right side of his face." ..."

The following quote from Samael Aun Weor is about "astral cells" (this could refer to parasites from the astral):

"In the third method I let go of my body and mind by closing and opening my eyes by means with an imagination as well as an explicit physical intention. I place my hands to my face. I pull them back a bit and then hold them on my head and for few seconds , or even for a few minutes, and then reduce them gently and slowly. I exhale slowly. Every time I exhale, get more and further away from my astral body... In the end, it is essential to utilize the vital fluid of nature, which is called vital breath. When you breathe out of your body's physical body and then leave it, you should breathe in your astral body, too in order that when you are simultaneously breathing inside and outside the bodily body you are becoming more aware of the plane of astral awareness."

Astral projection isn't an fad or a method of entertainment, it's a serious. Persons who are able to project their souls from their bodies may develop psychic abilities (such as psychic telepathy) or prophecy. They also interact with other people who are extremely wise and advanced beings from different dimensions or worlds.

Astral projection can be described as an event where one's mind departs from their physical body but is still in a state of rest. The mind is in contact with the body, however, more of a passenger rather than being its primary driver. The distinction between the body and the astral happens as consciousness expands from the body. While the physical body is breathing and continues to move, it is unable to more interact with the surrounding environment as well as receive any sensory signals from any external source to it. Consciousness projected beyond the physical body at all times regardless of whether you are asleep or awake but not everyone has the experience of Astral projection when at home (i.e. that is, in the absence of supervision).

It is considered to be a naturally occurring process. Sometimes, it happens without effort from the subject. In other situations it requires a large amount of practice, self-discipline and discipline. Astral projection can occur when a person is dying or sick, or their physical body has become weak. It can also occur when the person has a aware mind, which is active and developed. In all cases astral projection typically occurs during the night or when in states of semiconsciousness or unconsciousness (i.e. it is a state like sleep). If a person is a person with an advanced nervous system or nerve system very active, it could result in semiconscious state and eventually to astral projection.

Another reason for astral projection can be due to certain intense dreams. In these instances the person can experience severe psychosomatic symptoms while in the dream state, and may even experience death simulation. It can happen if the individual has strong unconscious parts that are suppressed in the daytime however they come out in semiconscious or sleep states (i.e. dream states). The cold components can manifest themselves in different forms of nightmares and dreams or in extreme psychosomatic signs.

There are other causes for astral projection. Certain individuals acquire the ability to travel through the astral while sleeping or even during their infancy. According to some occultists and the occult research groups they believe this is a significant method for consciousness to move between one dimension or plane to another. They assert that the phenomenon of consciousness is deeper than we imagine and can be an interconnection between dimensions or the planes of reality that may be near or even simultaneously.

Some experts suggest that any sudden action can trigger body and mind separation. In some instances the body can be sucked away by an inexplicably strong force. Experts say that when a person is using his body excessively and the body cannot more support itself and it begins to break down. In other instances, too many electric shocks, or numerous aggressive actions will cause the spirit of a person to split from his body.

In certain instances individuals' consciousness could disappear from his body without ever being moved at all. In this situation it is possible that the individual will be paralyzed , but "be" conscious throughout his head as well as throughout his body. This can be a scary situation as there isn't any exit from the location that this occurs. In fact, he's able to view himself in a completely free manner and observe all that is going on around him, but is unable to consciously aid himself in waking up or leave this state. In this situation the person's consciousness could be absent from his body, however the person is still conscious and able to perceive everything that is happening that is happening around him.

In other instances when a person is experiencing intense pain in his physical body and is not able to move or interact with the surrounding environment and his mind will become separated from his body in all circumstances. It can also happen if there is so much anxiety in his brain that they lose control over the whole nervous system throughout all of the body. In this case, both consciousness and the brain could be removed from the body nevertheless, they remain connected since communication happens between the brains of different people when still in the body. It is also possible that one's consciousness is temporarily removed from the body of the deceased individual or animal, and they are able to observe every aspect of the body.

There are many other cases where someone is experiencing what may appear to be the astral projection. The reason behind this is not the typical astral projection. In actuality, it could be something else from a different dimension or the plane of existence. Many believe that such instances could occur because people are unconscious due to extreme trauma or another type of shock. In this case, consciousness is able to leave its physical body at any time and could even be able to communicate with the surrounding environment without taking actions.

In addition, consciousness is tied to the physical body since the body's senses can be used by its senses. It does not mean consciousness is a separate entity from the body in these instances however the consciousness is still within the physical body. Consciousness gets sensory information from people and animals by using psychic powers including telepathy, clairvoyance and clairvoyance and more. Also, it observes general information on people and events in its area of focus or observes.

There are other instances where people escape their bodies in a state in which their mind is asleep however their brain is active but extremely tired. This is a frequent occurrence in children who are developing. In this case, consciousness departs its body as like it was floating in space. In these situations the degree of consciousness is not significantly higher than sleep, however the mind and its ability to make decisions are extremely tired. In this situation one cannot transmit his consciousness away from his body. He is unable to be anything other than observing his surroundings and get information regarding them via psychic abilities that permit the person to be aware both physically and mentally."

It seems that at the very least some people have been learning about astral projection through one of the numerous books about "The Law of One" that was channeled by the group called "Ra." Ra was the one who supervised the research in the 1960s and 1970s. The material is now accessible in diverse books, including Ra Material. One of the books available includes "The The Law of One" composed by L/L Research, a channel for Ra. The book provides information on astral projections dating from a young period of. I'll provide a few quotations from the book to illustrate what the Ra group saw astral projections

"Now we have some of this information that we believe needs to be corrected. The instrument was aware that the distortions in this instrument's perception of its capability to communicate with the person it communicates with and recall what happened during the session rendered this instrument unusable to continue communicating. We know that, due to flares of pain this instrument might cease to function. But, for any healing process the instrument should be prepared to be used. In order to be ready to refer to, it is essential that the device repeatedly try to contact with each set of painful flares until it's successful. If we could say so the amnesia that causes the device think that it has lost some of the sessions is due in part to the instrument not having a clear understanding of these attempts, and therefore not making them stronger.

To ensure that it can maintain contact through the distortions of this instrument We suggest it is beneficial to improve its capacity to accept messages by practicing visualizing the presence of this communication as if it were happening."

"Is you able to follow up on your inquiry?"

"Yes I have one. When I was doing healing was noted that the instrument became cognizant of people who were in this space/time reality throughout the process. It is our understanding that their presence assists in the ongoing contact with the instrument. Do you think someone could be aware without the other being present? Can you please clarify?"

"Yes there are a variety of ways to making contact with an individual. In order to proceed with the session the contact needs to be made by all present in your own particular time and space/time continuum. Contact can be made without anyone else talking. In order for the contact to take place your attention to be focused, and your energy full of passion. Without these two things the relationship will not occur."

"Is there any follow-up questions?"

"Yes I do have another. How long will it take to come to awareness during the healing process?"

"At this moment we do not talk about time or the length of time it takes to are aware of us in the healing process. At this point we recommend that each instrument engage in a rigorous concentration in order to increase its capacity to allow us to enter into its own reality/time continuum. This is the very first practice suggested in our guideline on communicating with others. We strongly suggest that every instrument do this as often as is possible and repeat the exercise at least twice a week."

Here's more details about astral projection:

"We have now explained that we have a clear knowledge of your time continuum/reality and the way that consciousness is created in that space and time reality, the way we can connect with you. We'd like to discuss how these connections are made within the healing process. Many have stated to your acquaintances and family members the possibility exists to "leave your body" or escape the body. Our understanding is that this is not true in the sense that If one, for instance was suffering from a fever or experienced discomfort in the body, and then experienced a temporary dissociation from the body during the treatment and later was aware of this happening and then realized that the instrument had projected. But, we've just discussed how it is confusing to view projections of the mind as being removed from one's body. But, there are various kinds of consciousness transfer that do not require leaving the body. One example is the transition of consciousness from a sleep state to a dream-like state. When this happens it is possible to appear asleep or asleep however, consciousness is awake and alert. In other situations consciousness could transfer from an region of the body to another. This is also a kind of projection that does not require leaving the physical body."

Chapter 10: The Complete Guide To Know About Psychic Protection

Do you ever feel like something is occupying your energy? It can be uncomfortable, invasive and at times even terrifying. It's in these scenarios that you require psychic protection. In this article we will cover all you need to know about the practice and practice of protection through psychics in a step-bystep method.

The most common method of psychic protection is the setting up of shields or mirrors that can send negative energy back to the person who is responsible for. There are other options also that involve the use of light with various frequencies, and the most important thing is White light, which does not just safeguards, but also cleanses. Some prefer to rely on guides and angels who offer them protection in the event of attacks on their psychic. However, in this chapter I'll demonstrate why you don't require anything else, and instead safeguard your mind with alternative methods, like improving your boundaries with the auric system and establishing your chakras correctly.

If you're experiencing a psychic attack, it indicates that a specific area the energy of you is open to attack. It is imperative to shut the energy door and raise your drawbridge to ensure that you are protected from being attacked.

One interesting thing that has been recognized by experts is that people who have powerful boundary energy, they generally do not require any psychic security in the first place. This doesn't mean that they don't face many challenges, or that their lives are perfect. But, in the same way, they're not victimized by psychic attacks.

This indicates that the need to protect does not arise if you're capable of containing your energy. This will ensure that your energy won't be readily available and can be used for the possibility of psychic attacks. In this way, you're in a position to break this cycle between victim and victim.

But how can this control be successful? One way is to set your chakras correctly. You can also participate in a series of grounding and centering exercises to improve your energy levels. Find out more about these practices.

Grounding and centering exercises

If you are looking to control your stress levels or shield yourself from psychic attack the practice of grounding and centering are extremely beneficial. Actually, when we talk about any energy or spiritual exercise, these two elements have a lot in common. When you do these exercises, you'll be able to feel the energy flow throughout your body. Additionally, you will also be able to control more of the energy. These exercises ultimately aid in bringing a sense of calmness and peace within. Another benefit of this type of exercise is the fact that they help make the participant aware of their physical, emotional and psychic boundaries. This way, you are able to easily construct your energy shields and take part in psychic protection.

If you do follow my suggestions I'd advise you to do these exercises daily A good practice is to practice for 15 minutes immediately after waking up and 15 minutes after you end your day and get ready for bed. There are a variety of ways to train your centering and balancing however for those who are just beginning the most effective method is to do breathing exercises.

What is the term Grounding?

With the hectic schedules everyone has it's easy to be overwhelmed by everything you must check off your list of things to do to accomplish in the day. Then there are those thoughts of the uncertain future. These thoughts can make a person feel disconnected from their daily life. This is where the concept of the idea of grounding can help.

In the process of grounding, you will be able to pull yourself back into reality and help you reconnect to the present. It instantly reminds you of the importance of staying present and present so that you're always aware of the events within you and remain alert. When you feel completely detached from everything happening at time, exercises that ground you can help you change your perspective and help you return to the present. It can also help you remain mindful.

What is the best way to Ground Yourself?

The exercise of grounding is fairly simple and you'll become more proficient at it through practicing. Begin by choosing a spot to lie down in a place in a space that is clear of distractions. Then, close your eyes. Start taking deep breaths. When you breathe out and in, you should focus on your breathing. You should be conscious and attentive to every breath you take and exhale that perform.

After a few minutes it will be easier to feel relaxed and you will begin to imagine the energy that is generated by your body colliding at the center before moving to the bottom. This can be done by visualizing the roots that grow out of your body. These roots continue to grow deeper into the ground. And they carry the energy along with the ground. As these roots expand and expand, the more you'll feel heavy as they are pulling you towards the ground. If you feel overwhelmed it is possible to imagine your spirit being pulled further and more toward your body. After a few minutes you'll feel totally relaxed as your body and your spirit are one. The next step to complete is to center.

What is the meaning of Centering?

If you've got an idea of what a grounding concept is and what it is, let's take a review of the second idea, which is centring. To understand this, consider the following situation :

You adhere to your schedule and then go to work throughout the day, you do to keep your boss satisfied and ensure that your clients are satisfied. You are in contact with a variety of people throughout your shift and all the time you try to put on a smile. However, there are times when you're dealing with a cranky customer or client to handle and they exhibit unsettling behavior. When your day comes to an end you are exhausted and exhausted, not just physically but also mentally and all you would like to do is lie at the television or sit down to Netflix with your favourite snacks.

Does this sound like your routine? That's what it sounds like to me! This is the reason why it is crucial for each person to learn to center themselves.

Energy is a universal phenomenon and everything is visible on the earth contains energy. When you travel through life, you share some of your energy , and continue to receive energy from other people. These exchanges of energy shouldn't be ignored. It is essential to monitor it someway in order to avoid the possibility that you'll be feeling overwhelmed by the negative energy of others, and this can affect your own spiritual well-being.

When you work on your centering technique and focusing, you restore the energy that you earlier passed onto others. In the process you eliminate the energy you received from those you have encountered. The advantage of this procedure is that it allows you to restore balance within your body, so that you are able to function more efficiently and efficiently, without feeling weighted down by anything.

What is the best way to center Yourself?

The first thing you must know prior to you begin to center yourself is the location of your energy center. There's a breathing routine that you have to complete, but before I go over what steps to follow, there's an more I'd like to explain to you. If you are doing the exercise of centering you want to visualize the energy gathering within your body as of an emerald ball. It is generally about the area around your navel. This is the reason why, when you breathe it is suggested to breathe through your diaphragm. If you don't yet believe in yourself for clarity of visualization, you need not be concerned - simply visualize the energy flowing towards the area you want it to flow towards. The process of developing or opening your psychic capabilities has been linked with the ability to visualize, therefore, you should never be able to put a stop to your imagination. If you make the most effective utilization of your creativity, and apply it with purpose, you recognize the energy that is within you , and ultimately discover how to shut down your inner critic in order to get the most out the abilities of psychics.

Start by closing your eyes , then taking deep, slow breaths. You must utilize your visualization as you breathe in. Imagine all the energy you've released into the universe and visualize it returning to you. As the energy returns and fills you it makes your soul feel full and give you an overwhelming feeling in your own.

When you exhale, try to think of getting rid of all the energy you have absorbed from others. Imagine the excess debris within you, and then just blow it away. This procedure is sure to ensure all the negative energy that blocks your energy flow has been gone and your body becomes neutralized. You will feel lighter and more relaxed than you did before.

If you're having difficulty performing, here's a good example of a visualization you can practice while performing breathing exercises. Imagine your energy center , and examine it in comparison to the empty cup. Imagine that your cup is covered by litter. Every time you inhale, visualize the litter moving further away, and then your cup filled with pure water. The water symbolizes your own energy and the litter is the energy of others you don't need. Also, you could imagine an idyllic garden. Each time you breathe, think of the new blooms appearing in the garden as you exhale. With each exhale, visualize the weeds getting sucked up.

Making the Psychic Shield

If you are feeling that your negative energies of other people constantly influences you, then it is important to learn how to construct psychic shield. In this article we'll examine the process of creating a shield in greater detail.

How do you define Shielding?

What should you do when you are outside the home during winter? You cover yourself with warm clothing, right? In the event that you don't, you'll to get sick from cold. Shielding is very similar to this one It's an act of defending yourself against negative energy that surrounds you. It protects you from wasting your energy, and protects you from energy-related attacks. When you build this shield of energy it helps you to put away any energies you are sure are not in your best interests and are likely to harm you. This means that no matter the number of negative people you're surrounded by your negativity will not be as detrimental to you that it did in the past. The chaos in your routine not going cause stress or cause you to burn out since you'll be able to shield yourself from negativity surrounding you.

At first the shielding process may appear as a daunting task, however don't let it deter you. Through practice and perseverance you'll soon be able to be able to master it like an expert. Then you'll see the powerful impact it could have on your mental and spiritual well-being.

How can you shield?

It's essential to calm yourself before practicing shielding however, it's fine if you don't. Simply ease your mind to relax by taking some deep breaths. This will help you gain clarity , and gradually bring feelings of relaxation.

It is the first thing to do closing your eyes. Be sure that you are in a location that is free of any distraction. Sit for a few minutes in stillness. In a few minutes, you'll experience a surge of energy in your body. If you don't, you must be focused upon your energetic center. Slowly and slowly take note of the energy that is inside you . It's pulsating and you can visualize it. When you feel you're full of energy, take some deep breaths.

Inhaling it is important be imagining that air fills your lungs while at the same simultaneously, engulfing you in positive energy. Repeat this process until you're feeling happy, and feel the positive energy within you.

Now, you must focus your positive energy to the task at hand. Continue to take deep breaths. When you exhale, now must imagine that the energy center within your body will open. After a few minutes you'll be able to feel that your energy center has fully opened. When that happens you must imagine that the energy emanating from the energy centre has begun to expand. Keep in mind that the energy expanding right now can be the exact energy source that is later used to create the shield. You need to make that happen by visualizing it.

If you are a beginner, and you shield for the first few times, take some time learning about the energy, This will make sure that the shield you construct is robust. Discover the various characteristics of your energy

What color is the energy?

What is the energy you are made of? Are you able to tell if it is liquid? Are you seeing translucent? Or is it something else completely?

Does it feel cold, or does it feel hot?

How do you feel your energy field is moving around?

The power of your shield is entirely on your ability to imagine. The following step is visualize the energy around you completely. One of the most crucial steps in making a shield that works is to concentrate on the purpose behind it. Your shield will stop only the energies that are not aimed at your health and wellbeing, and allows only those energies that do you happiness. This is a crucial aspect since it is the base of the shield. Keep in mind that it's okay that this step takes an more time as there is no reason to screw it up, don't you? The effort will be well worth it in the end So be strong and be patiently waiting until the shield forms.

Shields in various types

There are a variety of kinds of shields that could be made and we're going explore them in this article.

Bubble Shields. Let's begin by making the easiest shield. These are the most simple shields you can make for those who are new to the craft. It serves as a fine net that filters out energy precisely in the way you'd like it to. Empaths can use the shield in their everyday routine. However, be aware that these shields cannot work against telepathy.

What do you plan to build the bubble? It is essential to use your energy of grounding in the process. Inhale the amount of energy you require and imagine it as an enveloping bubble around you. Imagine that the bubble surrounds your entire body. The shield needs to be thought of as something that bounces and a thought in your head that, when someone throws something towards this shield it bounces off. If you'd like your experience to be different and imaginative, you could imagine the shield as having the same hue. If you're trying to defend yourself against severe attacks it is not the ideal shield.

Mirror Shields. You can see in the name unlike bubble shields the mirror shields are more durable, and if you encounter any attack at you, the shields will reflect and block it. In the process of creating this shield, it's advised to visualize the outside of it as a mirror and diamond-hard. The shield cannot be moved easily, and is, therefore far more robust over bubble-shaped shields.

If you're looking to build a mirror-like shield around yourself then you must imagine the energy that is inside your body and slowly transform this energy into an armor. Once it is in the spherical form and you are able to put all your attention on its surface. Imagine it as solid and reflective like the diamond. Remember that, like diamonds, when these shields are struck with a specific force and in the right position, they may be damaged.

Elemental Shields. The primary function they serve is to layer and are very effective at this. Mirror shields are typically static, but this does not happen for elemental shields. This is why they are their strength and flexible. The shields, as the name implies are able to draw energy from particular element. If you're able to construct them in the correct way they draw on the strength and essence of the element in question. However, it is essential to keep in mind the boundaries of that element when making the shield. The different types of shields made from elemental elements are as follows:

Wind Shields They are a must for any wind-driven vehicle. We've all witnessed how strong tornadoes or cyclones can be and that's the strength you'll get from these shields. In the event that your protection is of good quality and sturdy, it should comprise at minimum two layers in which each layer is moving in different directions.

Fire Shields In this case you need to imagine the flames surrounding the area you are. This shield is simple and is easy to keep up to help you empathize with psychic energy. If excessive energy is thrown at it at once it is a possibility for it to get overwhelmed. Another benefit for this type of shield is it lets those around you to feel comfortable in your presence due to the warmth that it emits.

Water Shields The water shields are extremely strong and impressive due to the strength of floods as well as tide waves. It is also a lively shield, similar to the two previous fundamental shields. The person who casts it will experience a feeling of cleansing as well as a sensation of cool. However, if the person does not enjoy water in general, or doesn't have an affinity to the element, the shield could make them feel nauseated.

Ice Shields Ice shields are not a product to be used by everyone. It is a natural way of sucking the heat from any type of energy. Anything that comes into close contact will be frozen.

Earth Shields - a sandstorm. This shield is extremely corrosive the natural environment. Imagine building this shield through visualizing the construction of a brick by brick. The downside is that it's not simple to maintain as it's a large shield.

I hope this article has given you a better understanding of the process for psychic safeguarding. If you're new to this, begin with the simple procedures and gradually work to the next level.

Chapter 11: Stabilize , And Sustain Your Gift

Someone who has psychic or emotional abilities (Empaths) has the unique ability to sense and feel emotions or feelings of other people. Empaths are very attuned to emotional surroundings of others but also other objects, locations and even animals. They are also able be able to discern and comprehend their thoughts. In turn, they are extremely sensitive to the energy of things and people.

Empaths can sense the feelings of others physical pain and symptoms hearing voices, seeing visions or even sense what other people think. They can also connect with animals, too. They can feel uneasy whenever they are overwhelmed by the presence of someone new within their surroundings. They will be able to tell that someone is threatening within the space or room the area they're. Beginning from the time they are infants, Empaths can sense the sentiments that their parents feel. They are able to tell whether their parents aren't feeling well.

Empaths cannot tolerate extreme fear, anger and hurt because the emotional energy they feel affects them in a negative way and are easily exhausted from these emotions. Empaths are often at a heightened level in certain situations or locations with sudden surges of intense negative emotions. Some refer to this as "getting caught up in your energies" which can become extremely stressful.

Emotional Empaths tend to be willing to help others however, they are more likely to get involved and their emotions in other people's issues. It is crucial to not get too involved in the feelings of other people.

It is important for Empaths to know their own self better, discover how to calm their minds as they learn about meditation, and improve their sense of intuition. They can to reduce their sensitivity, thereby shielding from excessive disturbance and preventing them from being completely exhausted.

Here are a few steps that will help Empaths to get the most out of their gifts:

Step 1: Make Friends With Your Sensitivity

Empaths are able to feel the feelings of others. They also can detect words and phrases are spoken by others subconsciously, which is known as "thought transmission". Empaths can also sense the emotional energy of others, which may influence them , causing them to feel tired. Therefore, making friends with your sensitivity is essential.

The emotions will always be present and you need to be able to manage them. It is crucial to realize that how you react to emotions is based on your personal beliefs about values, your upbringing, and values. Recognize that the negative emotions you experience are only temporary in nature They will fade away and transform. Begin by spending time with fellow Empaths to discover how they handle their sensitive feelings.

The way you see and respond to the sensitivity of others will also be influenced by the traits of your personality. For instance, extremely sensitive people tend to be introverted, shy and quiet. They are not a fan of crowds or huge crowds. It is normal for an empath when they are uncomfortable in a specific setting or environment, therefore they should learn to avoid situations that do not serve their best interests.

Step 2 - Find Balance in Your Energy

Negative energies can affect Empaths and deplete their energy. They need to be aware of those around them, their surroundings, where they go, how they behave and what events or situations cause powerful emotions. The Empaths have to protect themselves from negative energy.

Empaths must always guard their energy levels and maintain their sanity by eating healthy foods exercise regularly and taking enough rest. They must avoid circumstances and people who create negativity in their lives.

When Empaths feel overwhelmed by excessive emotions or energy during the course of their day, they must to figure out how to let go of the extra energy and not feel overwhelmed. An Reiki or EFT session is beneficial in this situation. It is beneficial to understand how to get their energy grounded by connecting to Mother Earth or Father Sun. They could also request Mother Earth or Father Sun to protect them from the negative energies that surround them.

For Empaths Also, it could be beneficial to wear healing crystals to guard themselves against being in the grip of negative emotions from others. In crowds they could utilize a grounding and protection stone to aid in separating.

Step 3 - Perform Self-Care

Empaths are known to devote all their attention and energy toward their beloved ones, without realizing the. They should be aware of their limits, and when it is time to stop and enjoy some "me time".

Empaths should establish healthy boundaries. Family members, friends and their loved ones might have abused them at one time. They are prone to giving too much and expect nothing to be returned. When they learn to establish limits, Empaths will protect themselves from being abused or depleted by others.

Empaths should learn to be able to say "No" whenever they need to and be able to adhere to their own decision-making. They should be aware when making acquaintances or accepting assistance from others, since they might be co-creating similar relationships in the future.

Step 4 - Care for Your Body

Empaths are prone overexert themselves beyond their limits without realizing. They must be aware of their bodies, minds and emotions to ensure they don't become exhausted.

The Empaths must be aware of their mental and physical health. They must take an effort to take time each throughout the day in order to replenish themselves. Regular exercise will aid in sleeping better in the evening and stay alert and positive throughout the day.

Empaths must be aware of their nerve system so as not to become overwhelmed by many emotions or energy sources in their lives. They should avoid watching news, or anything that triggers their emotions.

Healthy eating is essential for Empaths as it keeps them focused and grounded. They should stay away from processed food such as sugar, caffeine and coffee since these chemicals can cause them to become distracted.

In addition, they must maintain a sense of humor about themselves, as they are frequently influenced by the thoughts and feelings of others. If they don't have a sense of humor about themselves, they'll be constantly exhausted from the environment that surrounds them.

Step 5 Be Patient, Positive and persistent

Empaths are typically the type of people who wish to assist others in overcoming their issues. They are often able to solve problems of others without conscious of they are doing it. They must learn to be patient, positive and persevering.

If an Empath is engaged in healing or helping others They should only do it if they feel it is appropriate for them. It is not appropriate in order to make themselves feel better or feel like they are helping people.

One of the primary methods for Empaths to assist others is through applying their self-healing methods. If they feel exhausted it is best to do something that helps them feel more relaxed. There is no need to attempt to make the problems of others make them feel better, as it could drain the person even more.

Step 6 - Keep Learning

Empaths are inclined to save the world without realizing they are doing it. They must keep learning new techniques to avoid this behavior.

One of the most effective ways to improve their knowledge is by reading self-help books, as they are able to gain a lot of knowledge from people who were in their position. It is also possible to seek out a mentor who will help them deal the challenges they face.

One of the most effective ways to help an Empath to develop is by studying the people and events surrounding them. They should find out what's wrong and why a circumstance is how it is. This will help them avoid getting themselves drained and others in the future, by avoiding similar situations or individuals.

Step 7 - Create Boundaries

Empaths should learn to establish boundaries with other people. This can help them identify their personality and the things they can accept from others.

Empaths might also wish to seek out a counselor who can assist them in learning how to define limits in their lives.

Step 8 Step 8 - Be Honest with Oneself

Empaths must be truthful about themselves in regards to the situations. They aren't able to ignore the truth because they have to be aware of the reality of things and not hide from it.

Understanding the reality of things will help them understand what's happening in the world around them and what makes them are feeling the way they do in certain situations.

Step 9: Find a Job

Empaths may be looking for the ideal career path or job they are comfortable with.

It can allow them to channel their efforts into something they're passionate about and have fun doing it. They'll be able to be able to share their talents and talents to others in various settings.

10. Connect to Nature

Empaths can easily connect to nature because they are attuned to their surroundings. This means they are able to connect to nature on a personal level. If they're feeling overwhelmed or have experienced an unlucky day, it's relaxing to relax in the natural world. It is a refuge away from the stress of daily life, and helps them replenish their energy.

The most effective way to do this is to get outside and breathe in fresh air.

www.ingramcontent.com/pod-product-compliance
Lightning Source LLC
Chambersburg PA
CBHW050403120526
44590CB00015B/1800